PRAISE FOR *MARRIAGE MEETINGS FOR LASTING LOVE*

"In *Marriage Meetings for Lasting Love*, Mars and Venus meet on common ground at last. A wise, practical book for any relationship."

— Sam Krause, coauthor of
The Four Steps to a Successful Marriage

"This book says it all — in the most concise way possible! Newlyweds can use it to ward off trouble, and longtime marrieds can use it to get back on track. I highly recommend this manual for *any* couple who wants to build, maintain, or heal their relationship."

— Sarah Chana Radcliffe, MEd, author of
Raise Your Kids without Raising Your Voice and *The Fear Fix*

"Many married people try to convey the image that all is fine behind the front door. But everyone has issues they are living with and working on or not. This book can help you turn your challenges into a rewarding life together."

— Pamela Butler, PhD, author of
Self-Assertion for Women and *Talking to Yourself*

"A strong marriage is built not only on companionship and affection for one another but also on a bedrock of good common sense. This is a book of practical, good common sense and can be a boon to all those who wish to strengthen their marriage and relationship."

— Rabbi Berel Wein, coauthor of *The Legacy*

"Marcia Naomi Berger has made a brilliant contribution to couples everywhere. The elegant and coherent structure of her marriage meetings provides a much-needed, research-based ritual, which all long-term relationships require if they are to flourish. This book is full of straightforward relationship wisdom garnered from years of professional and personal experience. Bravo!"

— Timothy West, PhD, MFT, Certified Gottman Couples Therapist and founder of the Couples Clinic of Marin

"The ideas in *Marriage Meetings for Lasting Love* are laid out in a comprehensive and easy-to-follow style. Whether you have been married for two years or twenty, marriage meetings can only enhance your relationship."

— Francis Lu, MD, Kim Professor in Cultural Psychiatry, Emeritus, University of California, Davis

"When I was married, I never would have looked at this book. Now I'd jump on it. This book opened my eyes to a new way of relating. If I had known about marriage meetings back then, I'd probably still be married."

— Joel Blackwell, political consultant

MARRIAGE MEETINGS
for lasting love

MARRIAGE MEETINGS
for lasting love

30 Minutes a Week to the Relationship
You've Always Wanted

———◆———

MARCIA NAOMI BERGER

FOREWORD BY LINDA BLOOM

New World Library
Novato, California

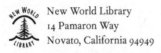

New World Library
14 Pamaron Way
Novato, California 94949

The material in this book is intended for education. It is not meant to take the place of individual diagnosis and treatment by a qualified medical practitioner or therapist. No expressed or implied guarantee of the effects of the use of the recommendations can be given nor liability taken. Names and identifying characteristics have been changed to protect the privacy of others.

Pages 185–89: Feelings Inventories and Needs Inventory, copyright © 2005 by Center for Nonviolent Communication, www.cnvc.org, email: cnvc@cnvc.org, phone: 505-244-4041.

Text design by Tona Pearce Myers

Library of Congress Cataloging-in-Publication Data
Berger, Marcia Naomi, date.
 Marriage meetings for lasting love : 30 minutes a week to the relationship you've always wanted / Marcia Naomi Berger.
    pages   cm
Includes bibliographical references and index.
ISBN 978-1-60868-223-2 (pbk.) — ISBN 978-1-60868-224-9 (ebook)
 1. Marriage counseling. 2. Couples therapy. I. Title.
HQ10.B47 2014
616.89'1562—dc23   2013041027

First printing, February 2014
ISBN 978-1-60868-223-2
Printed in Canada on 100% postconsumer-waste recycled paper

New World Library is proud to be a Gold Certified Environmentally Responsible Publisher. Publisher certification awarded by Green Press Initiative. www.greenpressinitiative.org

10   9   8   7   6   5   4   3

To David, my husband

Contents

PART III. COMMUNICATION SKILLS FOR EFFECTIVE MEETINGS

PART IV. TRANSFORMING RELATIONSHIPS WITH MARRIAGE MEETINGS

Foreword

What sets okay marriages apart from great ones? The quality of love and the depth of intimacy that the spouses enjoy. In this simple, straightforward guide, Marcia Naomi Berger shows couples how to enhance the quality of their time together and how to make it really count! Although many couples fear that their happiest days have already passed after one or two years of marriage, this book shows how the best can be yet to come!

In introducing the subject of marriage meetings, Berger emphasizes the importance of beginning by addressing less provocative and more manageable issues in order to gain experience and greater confidence in the process. Couples who take this advice will minimize the possibility of feeling overwhelmed and discouraged, which can happen when a couple's challenges are greater than their level of skill in dealing with them.

Marriage Meetings for Lasting Love helps partners avoid the pitfall of obsessing over problem issues by illuminating the importance of putting them aside temporarily, going "off-duty" and engaging in activities that bring greater play and ease into the relationship. Berger reminds us that cultivating a loving partnership isn't just about "working on our relationship"; it's also about cocreating experiences that bring pleasure and happiness into each spouse's life.

Berger emphasizes addressing feelings and needs responsibly rather than avoiding issues, and expressing appreciation and gratitude. Those practices are at the heart of this book as they are at the heart of great working relationships. They don't necessarily require massive amounts of time, and those reading this book can expect an immediate return on their efforts.

Making relationships a priority ultimately leads to each partner feeling valued and loved, and it enhances self-esteem in addition to strengthening the partnership. Many couples underestimate the amount of time and attention it takes to become sufficiently experienced and skilled in the art of effective communication. Holding weekly marriage meetings provides couples with an abundance of opportunities to practice the art of "conscious contact." Those who regularly practice Berger's four simple steps with a spirit of goodwill combined with full-hearted commitment will be abundantly rewarded.

Personally, I am a big believer in marriage meetings. My husband, Charlie, and I have been holding them for over thirty years. When we were still raising kids and juggling our two careers, carving out time to get together was a monumental challenge for us. We set aside part of every Monday afternoon while the children were in school and called the meetings our "sacred time." We kept a strict agreement to avoid any and all distractions and interruptions, including the phone or even the doorbell. Charlie's job was very demanding, and I feel certain that without these refueling stops, we would not have come through that challenging time with an intact marriage. Those meetings saved us.

Once he left his job, we went into business for ourselves, so in addition to the regular household chores that most families have, we now had a business to maintain. We set aside every Wednesday afternoon to build our business and to grab some personal connection time for emotional and sexual intimacy. We began to call these meetings "intimacy time." Creating this structure for our meetings was important for me because there was always so much to discuss — decisions to be made, workshops to schedule, and so on — and our personal time was the hot fudge sundae as dessert.

Our one-on-one meetings worked so well that we also instituted family meetings in which our kids could contribute to the agenda. Not surprisingly, they had a lot to say about a lot of things, including allowances, vacations, household chores, and curfews. While we had our share of tense moments, overall these meetings strengthened our family connections as much as our couple meetings strengthened our marriage. We continue to schedule these meetings when we go on family vacations, only these days our kids often remind us to hold them, and our grandchildren are there too.

Marcia Naomi Berger has nailed the essentials required for growing a great marriage, and I have no doubt that her book will inspire vast numbers to roll up their sleeves to follow her simple yet powerful steps. I am grateful to her for writing this book because I now have a practical, inspirational guide to recommend to my students and marriage-counseling clients. I encourage you to take her words to heart and give her suggestions a try. You won't regret it, guaranteed!

— Linda Bloom, MSW, LCSW, coauthor of
*101 Things I Wish I Knew When I Got Married:
Simple Lessons to Make Love Last* and *Secrets of Great Relationships:
Real Truths from Real Couples about Lasting Love*

Introduction

Marriage isn't what it used to be — which is a good thing! People have evolved and so has marriage. In a successful relationship today, spouses respect each other as individuals and also transcend their separate selves. The result is an amazing whole that is greater than the sum of its parts and nourishes both partners.

I believe in marriage. Some people, disillusioned by high divorce rates and unhappy unions, claim that marriage is obsolete. But now, like never before, you can create the marriage you've always wanted, a fulfilling one that fosters growth and vitality in both of you.

Society has altered radically, resulting in new expectations for marriage. Until recently, women needed husbands for financial support and men needed wives to do the homemaking. And virtually everyone needed marriage for sex and procreation. By and large, all this has changed.

Yet we continue to marry and expect lasting happiness. When disappointed, we tend to blame our spouse or the institution of marriage for not meeting a deeper need — the need to connect with each other emotionally and spiritually as well as physically.

To succeed in marriage, we need to catch up with our new expectations. Too many of us are relating in self-defeating ways, still focusing on physical aspects and ignoring the crucial need for a soul connection. To achieve this ideal, we must address the real issue: a lack of skills for a good twenty-first-century marriage.

Marriage meetings fill the gap. They offer a simple way for you to create an extraordinarily satisfying union that lasts a lifetime. Since 1998, I have been leading Marriage Meeting workshops for couples, making this tool available to professionals, and introducing it to clients in my private psychotherapy practice.

This book offers a practical way to gain a fulfilling marriage. By following its step-by-step instructions, you will increase romance, intimacy, and teamwork. When conflicts arise — and they do in any marriage — you will be able to resolve them more smoothly and respectfully.

If your marriage is already good, marriage meetings will keep it thriving. If you are facing unusual challenges, the meetings can help the two of you get back on track.

A good marriage fosters the growth and well-being of both partners, spiritually, emotionally, and physically. Each partner feels loved, cared for, and respected. Both husband and wife contribute their unique abilities to create a rewarding partnership.

Advice is plentiful. It's easy to pick up good ideas from many sources. The problem is that we soon forget the good advice and relapse into less healthy behavior patterns. The power of habit is simply too strong. The marriage meetings provide a frequent reminder to communicate positively. After you hold the meetings for a while, you will probably find that relating better in general has become second nature.

This book includes all you need to know in order to conduct effective marriage meetings: guidelines, step-by-step instructions, and positive communication techniques. Stories of couples included throughout the book are composite, general illustrative examples that do not represent any specific persons. Detailed descriptions of couples who have benefited from holding marriage meetings are featured in chapters 10 through 14 and show how applying marriage meeting concepts can enhance all kinds of relationships, whether they are well functioning or particularly challenged. Names and other identifying details have been changed to further protect confidentiality.

I do practice what I preach. My husband and I have been holding marriage meetings for over twenty-four years. I do not know how we would have stayed happy together without them. We reconnect every week by holding a meeting. We do not take each other for granted, because the meetings include a time to express appreciation. They also provide a platform that encourages us to say what each of us wants, collaborate on activities and projects, and clear up misunderstandings. Because the meetings bring closure, nothing is left hanging. Therefore, we don't hold grudges. Our meetings foster trust, romance, and intimacy.

You can expect to enjoy a ripple effect from marriage meetings. The warm feelings and optimism they generate will spread out to others in your life. You will start using positive communication skills in other relationships.

Like many of my therapy clients, I grew up in a home without role models for a happy marriage. My parents divorced when I was thirteen. In my positions as a child welfare worker, clinical social worker, psychotherapist, and family service agency director, I have always been drawn to activities that brought me into close contact with couples and families. I suppose that, unwittingly, I wanted to learn what I missed out on as a child — how to create a good marriage.

Every marriage has issues. A frequent complaint from couples is that they feel unheard by their partners. Marriage meetings keep them tuned in to each other. This proactive approach keeps small irritations from getting big and inspires each partner to value the other's good qualities.

The marriage meeting has four parts: Appreciation, Chores, Plan for Good Times, and Problems and Challenges.

Each part creates momentum for the next one. The first part, Appreciation, buoys you up for dealing with the next one, Chores, which takes energy at first. But you are likely to feel satisfied after cooperating while deciding who will do which tasks. The third part, Plan for Good Times, is usually a feel-good one because you plan a date with your spouse and decide on other enjoyable activities during this part of the meeting. The fourth part, Problems and Challenges, makes good use of the positive climate you've created for a fruitful conversation about any concern.

Are you ready to create the marriage you've always wanted? Let's get started!

Part I

——•◆•——

Preparing *for* Your Marriage Meetings

CHAPTER  I

Marriage Meeting Basics

OVERVIEW AND TECHNIQUES

A successful marriage requires falling in love many times, always with the same person.

— MIGNON MCLAUGHLIN

Can you imagine your partner and yourself holding weekly formal meetings? The idea might intrigue you, but will the meetings be effective? What if they turn into gripe sessions or a series of demands? Or if you're feeling optimistic, you might want to ask, "How do we get started?"

By reading this book before holding your first meeting, you will gain the confidence and know-how to conduct successful marriage meetings.[1]

THE MARRIAGE MEETING'S
FOUR-PART AGENDA COVERS ALL BASES

During Appreciation, each of you takes an uninterrupted turn to tell the other what you appreciated about him or her during the previous week. By doing this, you create a warm climate and positive energy for the rest of the meeting.

Chores is the business part of the meeting. Each of you says what you think needs to be done. You agree on priorities, timelines, and who will do each task. Teamwork is promoted and jobs get handled.

During the Plan for Good Times part of the meeting, you schedule dates for just the two of you, individual activities, and family recreation. Intimacy and romance are fostered, batteries get recharged, and family harmony is promoted.

In Problems and Challenges, each of you can bring up any concern — money, sex, in-laws, parenting, changing schedules, or something else. As you learn to resolve issues with kindness and respect, your marriage happiness will grow.

Some people ask whether it is all right to break the meeting into two sittings — for example, to conduct part of it before dinner and the rest after. If you do this, you are likely to compromise the meeting's effectiveness. As noted earlier, good momentum is generated by the order of the agenda topics. Picture a roller coaster. The forward motion gained on one part of the track carries the rider along to the next; stopping in the middle jeopardizes a good ride!

By following the guidelines that I offer here, you will prepare for effective marriage meetings.

How Long Does a Marriage Meeting Last?

Once you are routinely holding marriage meetings, you will probably be able to finish most of them within about thirty minutes. When you first start holding the meetings and are getting used to their structure and are developing communication skills, you can expect them to last a bit longer. This is true also for meetings held at any time when a topic calls for more discussion than usual, such as when a difficult challenge is being addressed.

In any case, adhering to a maximum time limit of forty-five minutes will help keep the discussion focused and productive.

Meet in a Private Place

Your marriage meeting is a private event for just the two of you. Ideally, hold your meeting at home. Choose a room where you both feel comfortable and where interruptions and distractions are unlikely to occur.

You may be tempted to hold the meeting at a restaurant while eating, making it part of an evening out. While that might sound like efficient multitasking, there are potential pitfalls to this approach. For example, just when you are on your way to resolving a situation you had to brace yourself to bring up in the first place, a server refills your water glass, or a friend stops by your table. Alas, you have lost your train of thought. Interruptions in a restaurant are likely to interfere with your concentration.

Kathy and Walter, along with other participants who attended the first session of a Marriage Meeting workshop, were told to conduct their first marriage meeting at home, where they could keep distractions to a minimum. During the second session, a week later, this couple reported that they had decided to hold their meeting in a restaurant because they liked the idea of combining it with a date. "We were interrupted too often to stay focused, and it was hard to enjoy the meal," Walter said. "Next time, we'll meet at home." His wife agreed.

Another reason not to meet in a restaurant is that you may experience stress during a marriage meeting, particularly when discussing challenging issues that arouse emotions. This is not a bad thing. Some conflict is normal in marriage. However, for good digestion, a relaxed mood is optimal. So avoid conducting a meeting while eating, even at home.

Do meet at home, at least until you establish a pattern of successful weekly meetings. Exercise self-control to minimize distractions. If your phone rings, let your answering system pick up the call. Resist the temptation to move wet clothes from the washer to the dryer. Meet after the children have gone to sleep or when they are otherwise occupied. If necessary, arrange for someone to supervise them.

Eventually, you may decide to allow an exception to the meet-at-home rule, such as meeting while taking a walk or driving somewhere. If you decide to vary the routine, you will be able to evaluate the pros and cons of doing so.

Meet Every Week

For best results, meet every week. You may be tempted to wait for a reason to schedule a meeting. As in any well-run organization, scheduling time to communicate on a regular basis is the best way to stay on track.

Perhaps you think that meeting regularly sounds cold and unromantic. But does ignoring concerns until they build to a crisis sound like a good way to foster a loving connection? On the other hand, does it make sense to talk to your spouse about issues whenever the spirit moves you, regardless of his or her availability to engage with you at that time?

Weekly meetings promote harmony and a sense of order. They free you from the pressure of too much accumulated mental clutter, because every week you will have a time to discuss your concerns constructively. The meetings prevent grudges from building up because they bring closure to lingering issues. They affirm that both of you value your relationship.

Where Will You Sit?

Where each of you sits affects the tone of a marriage meeting. Sitting next to each other on a couch or at a table fosters a sense of connection, as opposed to sitting across the room or table, which can create a confrontational mood. Marriage meetings are a wonderful way to increase collaboration. So sit close enough to feel like partners handling a project together.

A successful marriage meeting requires both partners to communicate their thoughts, feelings, wants, and needs. Physical touch can cause some blurring of boundaries and make it too easy to lose a sense of oneself and one's own priorities in the moment. Touch is wonderful at the right time. But cuddling up together while trying to communicate about your relationship can be a way of ignoring conflicts instead of addressing them constructively.

What to Talk About and in What Order

The four parts of a marriage meeting occur in this sequence:

1. Appreciation
2. Chores
3. Plan for Good Times
4. Problems and Challenges

Chapters 3, 4, 5, and 6 explain how to conduct each part of the meeting.

How to Conduct the First Few Meetings

The meeting should have a pleasant, supportive tone. For the first few meetings, it is best to avoid discussing sensitive topics. Do not use the time to make demands or criticize your partner. A good goal for each meeting is that it should inspire you to want to meet again a week later. If you have a big or long-standing issue you want to resolve, set it aside for after you have established a pattern of successful meetings and become comfortable using the positive communication skills, which are explained in chapters 7, 8, and 9.

When Yvette and Hank, a couple in their forties, held their first marriage meeting, all was well during the Appreciation, Chores, and Plan for Good Times segments of the meeting. But during

Problems and Challenges, Hank ignored the instruction to start with an easy-to-resolve challenge. He told Yvette, "I don't want you to give me the silent treatment when you get angry. I hate feeling ignored." Yvette was not yet ready to be confronted about this. She felt attacked and refused to participate in future marriage meetings. Had Hank begun with a smaller challenge, like by telling Yvette how hard he was finding it to stick to his diet and asking her to please hide the potato chips she buys so he wouldn't be tempted to eat them, she probably would have gladly complied and looked forward to future meetings.

If you keep your early marriage meetings light and enjoyable, both of you are likely to value them as a way of reconnecting and building trust for dealing with more serious concerns in later meetings.

WHY WON'T HE (OR SHE) INITIATE A MARRIAGE MEETING?

"I'll always have to initiate the meeting; otherwise it won't happen," wives say more often than husbands. This probably happens because female brains are typically wired for more sensitivity to relationships and verbal expression than males are. Don't worry about who initiates your meetings. The main thing is to make them happen.

People have other reasons to avoid scheduling meetings. Perhaps you have become comfortable with a less straightforward way of relating. Unhealthy patterns become entrenched over time and are difficult to reverse. But if allowed to continue, they can result in loneliness, emotional estrangement, depression, and resentment. More extreme difficulties that sometimes result from not taking corrective action when problems occur include domestic violence, alcohol or other substance abuse, medical issues, and even psychosis.

It is well worth the effort to adopt a new routine that can keep your relationship on track. Be optimistic and willing to experiment.

How to Overcome Reluctance
to Schedule a Marriage Meeting

You may be thinking things like "We're too busy to meet" or "There's no one to watch the children, and after they go to bed we're exhausted."

Ask yourself, "Do I dislike the idea of meetings in general?" If holding one with your spouse sounds too much like work, think of it as investing energy in your marriage to keep it *working* well. Surely, you can make a plan for child care or for an activity that keeps the children busy behind a closed door for less than an hour. Are there other ways to alter your routine to make time for a marriage meeting? Perhaps an earlier bedtime for the children? Or a restorative nap or other relaxing activity for you before meeting if you are "running on empty."

Other factors that may prevent you from scheduling a marriage meeting:

- You fear that your spouse will criticize you and demand that you change.
- You are holding on to one of the marriage myths that will be debunked in chapter 2.
- Your spouse refuses to hold a marriage meeting.

Do not let any of these concerns interfere with scheduling marriage meetings or using the recommended communication techniques for them. After finishing this book, you will know how to conduct effective, respectful meetings. Even if one partner will not participate in the formal meeting, you can still use marriage meeting techniques effectively. A wife reported that after she and her husband learned how to conduct marriage meetings at a workshop, he refused to hold them. She adopted what she had gleaned from the Appreciation teaching, making sure to compliment him every day. She reported that both felt better about their relationship as a result.

He became more relaxed, fun to be with, and supportive. When one of you changes, your marriage can benefit.

RETRAINING YOUR BRAIN FOR SUCCESSFUL COMMUNICATING

Change takes time and practice. If you practice using the skills described in this book, they will come naturally to you in time. It takes time to change any habit, including how we communicate. To recognize the power of habits, try this: Clasp your hands so that your fingers interlace. Look at them, then separate your hands and interlace your fingers again, but the opposite way, with your other thumb on top. Which way feels more natural? Does the "different" way feel awkward, strange, or wrong?

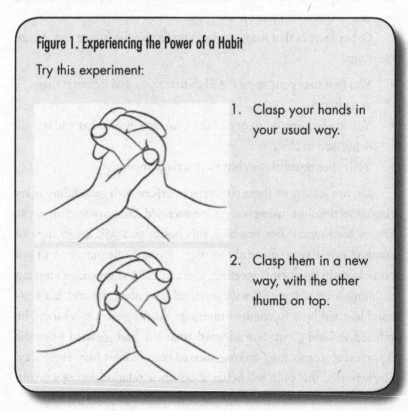

Figure 1. Experiencing the Power of a Habit

Try this experiment:

1. Clasp your hands in your usual way.

2. Clasp them in a new way, with the other thumb on top.

Similarly, parts of marriage meetings may feel unnatural at first. But if you persist, your relationship is likely to benefit. Isn't that worth about thirty minutes a week? Meet at a time that works well for both of you. Remember to stick to a time limit of forty-five minutes at most. Doing so will help maintain a positive focus and prevent fatigue.

DON'T STAND ON CEREMONY

You may agree to meet every Monday at 8 PM. But if your schedule, like mine, changes somewhat from week to week, you can vary the day and time you meet. I might ask my husband, "Would you rather meet Wednesday or Thursday evening next week?" I don't mind being the usual initiator, because our meetings bring clarity and good feelings to both of us.

By keeping an upbeat tone during the early meetings, you can reduce possible resistance from your partner or yourself, even if you have to "fake it before you make it." Agree to start light. Focus on the positives. In the Problems and Challenges segment, remember during initial meetings to bring up only issues that are easy to resolve. Concentrate on fostering harmony and goodwill. Eventually you will feel ready to tackle heavier matters. Equip yourselves with communication skills — which you will read about in chapters 7, 8, and 9 — before holding your first meeting.

TIPS FOR LONG-TERM SUCCESS

- *You can plan in advance or wing it.* If you choose to plan ahead, you can use the Marriage Meeting Agenda summary in Appendix A as a guide (see page 179). Write down the specifics you want to discuss during the meeting, including unfinished topics of discussion from a previous meeting. You can decide whether or not to communicate your personal agenda to your spouse before a meeting, either verbally or by sharing your notes. Some people do fine with a more spontaneous approach, writing little or nothing in advance of the meeting. It is fine to experiment. Do what works for each of you.

- *Bring your appointment book, notepad, and electronic or other organizing system.* During the Chores part of the meeting, you may agree to buy lightbulbs, call a plumber, or clear out some clutter from the garage. During the Plan for Good Times part of the meeting, you might offer to make reservations for dinner or a play. Writing down what you agree to do will help you remember and keep your commitments.

- *You can decide informally who speaks first.* Whenever possible, let the less verbal partner speak first regarding topics covered in your marriage meetings. This helps her or him to share ownership of the meeting with the more verbal one. Reflect back what you hear your partner saying when appropriate, using the active listening communication skill (discussed in chapter 9). Both partners' contributions to the meeting should be acknowledged.

- *Consider, if relevant to your situation, that it might be time to seek outside help.* Take an honest look at your relationship. If you know that issues are present that prevent you from creating the climate of safety and trust that is necessary for an effective marriage meeting, consider consulting a professional who is skilled in assisting with relationship issues. Such a person can help you move past obstacles and toward healthy, positive ways of communicating.

- *Be willing to dive in if your relationship is basically healthy.* If you are uncertain about whether you and your partner are ready for marriage meetings, try holding one after finishing this book. If you can follow the guidelines for meetings and use the techniques for positive communication, continue to hold weekly meetings. With practice, you are likely to do fine.

- *Stick with the program and meet every week.* In any relationship, there is always room for growth. If a relationship is not growing, the opposite is happening. When you conduct effective marriage meetings every week, your communication will continue to get better and better. After holding one or two meetings, you may feel tempted to skip one, or to wait for a reason to schedule a meeting. But missing a meeting can easily lead to missing another, and so on, until you have lost the drive to meet at all. Figure 2 (see page 14) shows the cyclical nature of the marriage meeting process, which is most effective if you meet every week.

A FINAL NOTE ABOUT GUIDELINES

Adhere to the guidelines in this chapter for conducting marriage meetings, at least for your first few meetings. If you find that a particular rule doesn't work well for you, talk about it and suggest a possible modification.

For example, the rule about not eating while conducting a marriage meeting fits for my husband and me. We also have held family meetings, and the rule about not eating applies for them too. However, when our son was an active teenager he objected to having to hang around after dinner for a meeting. He suggested this compromise: my husband and I would eat dinner without him, after which he would join us at the table and eat during the meeting. For this situation, we allowed eating while meeting.

Each of us is an individual; one size does not always fit all. If you find, after trying for a while, that a particular guideline does not work for you, experiment. Your goal is to reconnect with your spouse by having successful marriage meetings. Do whatever it takes to make this happen.

Figure 2. Marriage Meetings: A Cyclical Process

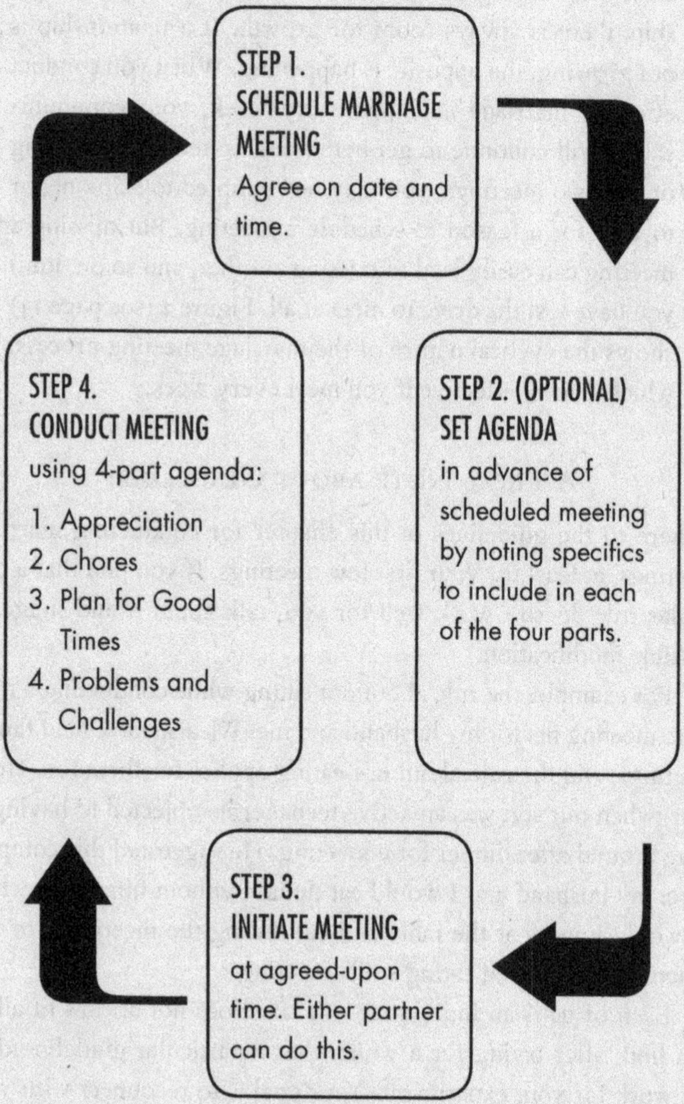

STEP 1.
SCHEDULE MARRIAGE
MEETING
Agree on date and
time.

STEP 4.
CONDUCT MEETING
using 4-part agenda:

1. Appreciation
2. Chores
3. Plan for Good
   Times
4. Problems and
   Challenges

STEP 2. (OPTIONAL)
SET AGENDA
in advance of
scheduled meeting
by noting specifics
to include in each
of the four parts.

STEP 3.
INITIATE MEETING
at agreed-upon
time. Either partner
can do this.

Regardless of how you may decide to alter guidelines to fit your unique circumstances and situation, for satisfying, successful marriage meetings, please remember to follow the agenda in the order shown in figure 3.

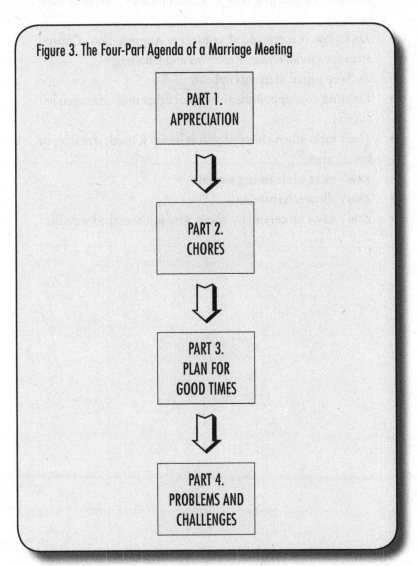

Figure 3. The Four-Part Agenda of a Marriage Meeting

PART 1.
APPRECIATION

PART 2.
CHORES

PART 3.
PLAN FOR
GOOD TIMES

PART 4.
PROBLEMS AND
CHALLENGES

DOS AND DON'TS FOR PREPARING
FOR A MARRIAGE MEETING

- *Do* meet weekly.
- *Do* limit the meeting time to a maximum of forty-five minutes.
- *Do* follow recommended sequence: Appreciation, Chores, Plan for Good Times, Problems and Challenges.
- *Do* keep initial meetings upbeat.
- *Do* bring your appointment book or other time-management system.
- *Don't* meet when either of you is hungry, tired, irritable, or intoxicated.
- *Don't* meet while eating a meal.
- *Don't* allow interruptions.
- *Don't* stand on ceremony about who initiates the meetings.

CHAPTER  2

Debunking Marriage Myths

There is nothing either good or bad, but thinking makes it so.
— SHAKESPEARE, *Hamlet*

If your partner tells you, "We have a problem," does your chest tighten? Do you forget to breathe? What goes through your mind? "A problem! Agh! Does that mean he (or she) will leave me? Is our relationship doomed?" Do you jump to the conclusion that something is terribly wrong with the two of you as a couple, so wrong that it may be impossible to fix?

If this sounds like you, you are probably being duped by a harmful marriage myth.

What you think a good marriage looks like will greatly influence how you feel about and behave toward your partner. This chapter focuses on some common false beliefs that cause unhappiness in marriage, and it offers a more realistic viewpoint for each of them. By replacing harmful myths with truths, you will develop a mindset that fosters successful marriage meetings and increases your happiness.

Destructive Marriage Myths

- A good marriage has no problems.
- You shouldn't have to work on a marriage.
- My spouse should know how I feel and what I want; I shouldn't have to say it.
- I shouldn't have to settle for less; I deserve better.
- In a good marriage, all problems get resolved.
- It is important to keep the peace at any cost.
- Love is all you need.
- A weekly marriage meeting can save *any* marriage.

MARRIAGE MYTH #1:
A GOOD MARRIAGE HAS NO PROBLEMS

A happily married couple shouldn't have problems, right? The truth is that conflict is present in any marriage. Our challenge is to deal with differences constructively.

Whether because of the fairy tales we grew up with or because schools teach little or nothing about the realities of marriage, many people think that in a good marriage a couple is not supposed to have any problems. They will pretend all is rosy until the stress of keeping their feelings inside builds to the point where it comes out harmfully.

Here are a few signs that may indicate you are ignoring a relationship issue: Your sex life is not good. Your child is too quiet or too aggressive. You think your partner doesn't love you. One of you is depressed, angry, or jumpy. You may find that you or your partner is drinking, eating, or gambling excessively.

Each of us has wants and needs — which don't always mesh with those of our mate. When we try to ignore what keeps us upset for too long, it can erupt like a volcano. Your particular challenge may concern intimacy, parenting, sex, money, in-laws, work, or something else.

Do not wait to deal with anything that puts your relationship at risk. Marriage meetings provide a safe, sure time to talk about what's on your mind. You get to reconnect with each other lovingly, to nurture yourselves and your relationship. You maintain the good feelings by dealing with small irritations before they grow into big ones.

The Potential for Conflict Exists Everywhere

Marriage and relationship educator Ellen Kreidman, PhD, gives a simple example that shows how the potential for conflict exists in any marriage, by referring to one small room: the bathroom.[1] One spouse wants the toilet paper to unroll from the top; the other wants it to unroll from the bottom. One leaves the toilet seat up; the other wants it down; one likes a sparkling-clean sink; the other leaves hairs or specks of makeup in it. One likes the door open; the other insists on privacy. And so on...

If you're thinking separate bathrooms, I'm with you! But that is not always possible. Still, by being creative and resourceful, you can often come up with ways to lessen annoyances.

The Risk of Concealing Differences

Lilly and Jonathan illustrate the danger of taking too long to identify and deal with a sensitive issue. Still childless after eight years of marriage, they finally adopted a baby girl. When Lilly first met Jonathan, she admired his take-charge manner. She felt protected by him. Soft spoken and diplomatic, she acquiesced to him on most matters.

Lilly's parents had fought a lot and eventually divorced. She didn't want this to happen to her. She believed it was important to go along with her husband on most matters in order to keep the peace. Before they became parents, he encouraged her to give up her career as a hospital nurse to stay home with their child at least until kindergarten.

Lilly thought this was a small price to pay for having her dream of motherhood come true. She squelched her doubts about giving up the work she loved and went along with Jonathan's idea for her to be a full-time mother. She told herself that it was the right thing to do.

But after two years at home, Lilly thought she would lose her mind. She loved her little girl, but she sorely missed the hustle and bustle of her hospital work, interacting with colleagues, and caring for patients. She also missed the salary, which she had been free to spend as she chose. Now she earned nothing. When Jonathan objected to a small purchase she made, he justified his right to do so by saying, "I'm the breadwinner." Lilly felt her chest tighten at such times. Wanting to keep the peace, she would say, "I'll take it back."

Lilly Pretends All Is Well until It Is Too Late

In public, Lilly played the part of a smiling, contented wife and mother. Privately, she began to feel distant from her husband. She lost interest in sex. She resented him but said nothing. She felt ignored and invisible — until she served a stunned Jonathan with divorce papers.

Is Jonathan a villain? Lilly shared none of her frustration with him. Should Jonathan have read her mind? Either partner might have saved their marriage by initiating an honest conversation. Jonathan could have asked his wife whether something other than her "headaches" was causing her to withdraw sexually. She could have told him about her unhappiness and said what she really wanted, even if she felt selfish or guilty.

This couple might then have found ways to compromise, perhaps by agreeing that she would return to work on a part-time basis. Lilly might have suggested to Jonathan that it would be fair for each of them to have a certain amount of money to spend with no questions asked, regardless of who earned it. By talking it out with honesty and mutual respect, they might well have created a way for practical solutions to emerge, for trust to grow, and for the return of emotional and physical intimacy.

MARRIAGE MYTH #2:
YOU SHOULDN'T HAVE TO WORK ON A MARRIAGE

Fairy tales promote the effortless happily-ever-after marriage myth when we are at an impressionable age. Later we view romantic movies and read novels with happily-ever-after endings.

As a result, many adults hold unrealistic expectations about marriage. They spend more time maintaining a car — checking tire pressure, changing the oil, and getting the recommended inspections — than they spend on keeping their most important relationship in good working order.

Obviously, we humans are more complicated than cars. We have infinitely complex bodies to maintain. We also have feelings, different ways of thinking, different hopes and dreams. And then, when you put two of us together...

Some people resist the idea of a formal meeting with their spouse. They think it sounds like *work*. Why not just talk about things as they come up? Talking on the fly sounds very nice, and that is fine if you are able to do this effectively. But you might want to mention something when your partner is watching television, reading a book, or is otherwise occupied. You might be waiting for a right time that never comes. And if you do bring up a sensitive matter when it's the last thing your spouse is in the mood to discuss at the moment, you might feel like you have entered a minefield. Similarly, your spouse may want to discuss a concern when you are busy. It is easy to take one's partner for granted, to forget to express appreciation. Chores can pile up or not be handled well. You may forget to plan dates and other enjoyable activities. By scheduling a time for a marriage meeting, you will get to reconnect every week. Weekly meetings foster direct, positive communication that addresses concerns at a time when both of you are likely to be receptive. You get to feel appreciated and valued, gain a smoother-running household by coordinating chores, and add romance by planning dates. Issues are resolved and challenges are met before they escalate into crises and grudges.

Romance *can* continue throughout your marriage, but not automatically. The payoff from investing in periodic maintenance on your relationship is that the two of you can continue to enjoy love, intimacy, and passion. Together, you can create and maintain a fulfilling marriage that lasts for the rest of your lives.

MARRIAGE MYTH #3: MY SPOUSE SHOULD KNOW HOW I FEEL AND WHAT I WANT; I SHOULDN'T HAVE TO SAY IT

"I shouldn't have to tell him. He should know what I want," Cindy thinks. She believes her husband should know when she's in the mood to go out for pizza, not sushi, and vice versa. He should know what she wants for her birthday. He should know what turns her on sexually. She wonders how he can be so clueless, but she doesn't say a word.

Actually, there *are* people who are able to get their needs met without saying a word. They are called infants. A mother learns to read her baby's cues. She soon knows which kind of crying means "I'm hungry," "I'm tired," or "I'm uncomfortable; I need my diaper changed." She understands which body movements and facial expressions say "I'm scared," "I'm happy," and "I want that."

Adults who find partners who can read their minds exist in fairy tales and romantic movies. There, charmed couples don't need to be told how to give the perfect kiss, gift, and massage. What do these examples of mind reading have to do with real-life adult relationships? Very little, even in the best of marriages.

Usually the best way to feel understood by your partner is to clearly communicate what's on your mind kindly and respectfully. Even the most sensitive, intuitive spouse cannot read your mind, any more than you can expect to read his or hers. Yes, in a good relationship there will be some tuning in to each other. Just don't expect miracles.

If your self-expression was stifled when you were young, you will have some catching up to do as you learn to feel more comfortable saying what is true for you. This is okay. Doing so will become easier and easier as you continue to practice speaking up, using the communication skills described in chapters 7, 8, and 9.

MARRIAGE MYTH #4:
I SHOULDN'T HAVE TO SETTLE FOR LESS; I DESERVE BETTER

A woman wanted to get married. According to a widely circulated, word-of-mouth tale, here is her story: She met many men but was always disappointed. None of them had the combination of traits she felt she deserved. Despairing, she consulted a famous rabbi, Menachem Mendel Schneerson, the Lubavitcher Rebbe who was respected around the world for giving sage advice to whoever sought it. She told the Rebbe that she wanted a man who was always kind, considerate, generous, sensitive, assertive, a good listener, handsome, healthy, reliable, and responsible, and who would be a good provider and a good father to the children she hoped they would have.

"I'm afraid I'll never find such a man," she added.

"Certainly, you can find him," the Rebbe replied. "You can find him in a novel."[2]

In real life people have imperfections. (Yes, you too!) So when your partner disappoints you, ask yourself how important it is in the grand scheme of things that he or she behave exactly as you would like and possess only excellent character traits.

For example, you may have a husband who is a considerate, responsible partner who has a great sense of humor and other traits you value. It happens, though, that you love receiving flowers from him, but he rarely gives them because he thinks they are a waste of money. Do you want to kvetch and whine that you shouldn't have to "settle" for this "inconsiderate cheapskate"?

What if you are annoyed by your wife's habitual lateness? Yet you value her joie de vivre, creativity, helpfulness, and other fine traits. Will you grumble that you deserve better and think that if she really loved you she would be on time?

Instead, let go of unrealistic expectations. Buy your own flowers or live without them. Work around her lateness when it's not crucial to be somewhere on time, and tell her in advance when it really matters. Negotiate creatively; see chapters 7 and 9 for how to do this. Appreciate your partner's strengths and work around the limitations, and hope your partner will do the same for you.

If your relationship is basically healthy, you are not settling in the sense of accepting less than you deserve. You are *settling down* into living in harmony with your spouse. You have a marriage that is reality based. It is less than 100 percent perfect. It's real life.

MARRIAGE MYTH #5:
IN A GOOD MARRIAGE, ALL PROBLEMS GET RESOLVED

During my early workshops, I used to say that couples can resolve virtually any problem by holding a weekly marriage meeting. One wife present who had been married for fifty years blurted out, "That's not true. Many problems can't get resolved."

According to psychologist and author John Gottman, she was right. His groundbreaking research revealed that a whopping

69 percent of problems in marriage do not get *solved*.[3] His good news, though, is that many problems can be *managed*. Gottman states that couples can live with unresolvable conflicts about perpetual issues in their relationship if the issues are not deal breakers.

Simply put, it is not the presence of conflict that stresses the relationship; it is the manner in which the couple responds. Positive, respectful communication about differences helps keep a marriage thriving.

Here is what I actually meant when I said couples can resolve virtually any problem by conducting marriage meetings: The meetings foster a spirit of goodwill and acceptance, a live-and-let-live, respectful attitude that allows partners to be themselves. The process results in the ability to minimize or *manage* conflicts that may not be resolvable.

Unresolvable Conflicts Do Not Have to Be Deal Breakers

Here are a few examples of unresolvable conflicts that you can probably learn to live with, assuming you get along well most of the time:

- You think your spouse is too strict (or too lenient) with the children.
- You are irritated by your partner's habitual lateness.
- Your partner has an okay job, but you wish he or she were more ambitious.
- Your spouse leaves crumbs on the counter even though you've said you don't like that.
- Your spouse is forgetful.

How can you accept the quirks and habits of your partner that have been bothering you for some time despite your efforts to change unwanted behavior? Look at the big picture. All in all, are you glad to be married to this person? If yes, do you want to keep carping and become a source of irritation to your spouse, or do you want a happy marriage?

Ask yourself, "Am I so perfect?" In healthy relationships, partners accept their mates' foibles as part of a package that is precious.

Certainly, you may address some of these concerns during marriage meetings. Even if neither partner is likely to change much of what irks the other, both of you will get to express yourselves constructively. You can expect to feel heard and understood. You may gain small improvements.

For example, Lew is bothered by the casual approach of his wife, Ellie, to dressing for social and business occasions. During the Problems and Challenges part of their marriage meeting he tells her, "I want us both to look great at the dinner party my boss invited us to. I know you like to dress comfortably, but please wear something especially nice Saturday night. I like how classy you look when you wear earrings and maybe other jewelry too." He adds for emphasis, "This is really important to me, and for us, because I want that promotion." Of course, after Ellie complies, he will generously express his appreciation.

How to Manage Conflicts That Are Not Deal Breakers

During the Problems and Challenges part of your marriage meetings, say what's on your mind. If you know a situation is coming up soon in which you want your partner to behave in a certain way, this is a good time to ask for that. In the previous example, Lew told Ellie he would like her to dress up for a specific event. You can do the same regarding what you want your partner to do differently. Focus your comments on something fairly easy to change, especially during your first four to six marriage meetings.

Character traits are not likely to change, at least not without a great deal of effort. Lew did not ask Ellie to start dressing better all the time. That would have been unrealistic. Her careless approach to what she wears is an entrenched habit. He is learning to live with that because he loves Ellie regardless and appreciates her many fine qualities.

Lew realizes he's not perfect either. He appreciates Ellie for putting up with his forgetfulness and for finding ways to work around it. Lew is minimizing their conflict by *managing it*. He is encouraging his wife to dress better when it really matters to him. He does this when he has her full attention during their marriage meetings.

Keeping Your Expectations Realistic

Maybe your partner will agree to change. If so, wonderful! Just understand that our basic nature and character traits are likely to remain the same. So don't expect an introvert to become the life of the party, a frugal person to become a big spender, or a sensitive person to become thick-skinned.

However, behaviors that have not become habits can be fairly easy to change — if the person wants to. The key word is *want*. Your partner may or may not want to change. You may have heard this joke: "How many psychotherapists does it take to change a lightbulb? Just one — but the lightbulb has to *want* to change."

Long-standing habits take more effort and time to change. If your spouse agrees to change one, be glad. Also be patient. When your partner makes an effort, let the compliments flow anytime and especially during the Appreciation part of your marriage meeting. If you see no progress, and you think your partner will accept a gentle reminder, offer it during Problems and Challenges.

What if the change still does not happen? If your partner's fault is not a deal breaker, strive to accept what you cannot change. While teaching a class on a different topic a couple of years ago, Rabbi Joseph Richards commented off the cuff, "People are annoying. So find the person who annoys you least and marry that one!" All of us laughed, probably because he had voiced a truth that is rarely acknowledged. The lesson is to keep irritations in perspective. Look at the big picture.

Some Unresolvable Conflicts May Be Deal Breakers

Still, it can be lifesaving to recognize when a conflict is severe enough to cause a couple to end their marriage. Here are some examples of conflicts that are deal breakers for many, but not all, couples:

- One wants children; the other doesn't.
- One wants quality time with a partner who is a workaholic and comes home mainly to sleep.
- A partner is unwilling or unable to give up an addiction, such as to alcohol, drugs, or gambling.
- A partner is unfaithful.
- A partner is emotionally or physically abusive or both.
- Partners' values are too different for them to agree on major issues, such as who will work, where to live, and how to spend leisure time.
- Religious differences, including about the faith in which the children will be raised.

Although these conflicts can end up being deal breakers, you may still want to save your marriage. The more difficult challenges are likely to require additional effort, such as seeking individual or couple therapy to help you communicate more constructively or to set realistic goals and work toward achieving them.

If you and your partner are willing to hold marriage meetings, first conduct several low-key ones with plenty of appreciation. Keep the early meetings positive and light. If you are able to establish a pattern of successful meetings, then after four to six of them you can bring up a serious concern. This calls for patience, and the wait may sound like a long one. If necessary, you can unburden yourself in the meantime by talking with a trusted friend, therapist, or other objective confidant.

During a later marriage meeting, you can bring up more sensitive topics, by saying, for example, "I'm concerned about your lateness," or "I've noticed that you've been putting on weight; I'm worried about how this might affect your health." You can express your distress about your spouse's drinking, drug use, abusive behavior, or something else. Use the positive communication skills described in chapters 7, 8, and 9. If a challenge you want to discuss seems too daunting for the two of you to deal with on your own, consider getting outside support to help you address it constructively.

A Deal Breaker for This Couple: Infidelity

It may feel reassuring to know that most conflicts are not deal breakers, but it is also important to know when a conflict creates more stress than a partner can bear, such as when it threatens one's mental or physical well-being. A situation that one person can accept might be a deal breaker for another person. Each of us knows what we can and cannot tolerate.

For example, Nicki recognized when a marital conflict became a deal breaker for her. She wanted to be the perfect mother to her baby girl. Cliff loved their baby but thought Nicki was giving her too much attention. He felt neglected; especially when Nicki said she was too tired for sex.

Cliff turned to Kim, who had been one of Nicki's bridesmaids, for comfort. Still single, Kim never expected to get involved with a married man and certainly not with her friend's husband. Yet she found Cliff attractive and enjoyed his attention. They began meeting for coffee occasionally and confiding in each other.

When Nicki found out, she was upset. Cliff assured her that he and Kim were strictly platonic. Suspicious, Nicki checked his emails and found messages in which he wrote to Kim that he loved her and felt more connected to her than he had ever felt with anyone else.

When Nicki confronted Cliff, he was remorseful. He agreed to stop contacting Kim. When Nicki learned a month later that he was still seeing her, she feared their marriage was over. She told Cliff that she wanted the two of them to talk things over with a therapist. He told Nicki that wouldn't be necessary, because he loved only her and would break it off with Kim for good. Nicki sensed he was lying. She became depressed and anxious. She had difficulty sleeping. When she discovered that Cliff and Kim had spent an afternoon at a motel, she gave him an ultimatum: either they would begin couple therapy or the marriage would be over. When he refused, she filed for divorce.

Nicki was unwilling to tolerate Cliff's betrayal. She was suffering physically and emotionally. His infidelity became a deal breaker for her.

MARRIAGE MYTH #6:
IT IS IMPORTANT TO KEEP THE PEACE AT ANY COST

How do you know when you are closing your eyes to a sensitive issue because you want to keep your relationship pleasant?

First, gain awareness about what is upsetting you; then deal with it. If you are not conscious of what is wrong, how can you do anything about it? You can become aware that something may be amiss in your relationship by noticing changes that occur in your thoughts, feelings, behaviors, and bodily sensations. You may find yourself complaining and feeling less tolerant of your partner's shortcomings. You may feel unappreciated and unloved. Try to understand what these changes mean. If you realize that a conflict exists, think about how to deal with it constructively.

Failing to Address a Conflict Can Put a Relationship at Risk

As described earlier in this chapter, Lilly unconsciously blamed her husband, Jonathan, both for her feeling trapped at home with her child and for being unreasonably critical about her spending. She noticed that her chest tightened whenever he expressed disapproval of her for buying something he considered unnecessary and when he would move toward her in bed. She lost interest in sex and realized, "I no longer feel close to him." Seeing no way out of her misery except to leave him, she finally asked for a divorce.

Making Waves Can Save a Marriage

Lilly might have saved her marriage by asking herself these questions: "Why do I feel distant from Jonathan? What do I dislike about our relationship? What am I unhappy about in my life? What would it take to make me happy?"

She might have realized, "I'm feeling angry at Jonathan for trying to control me." She might then have opened up her world by asking herself what it would take to make her happy.

After coming up with answers to these questions, Lilly could have initiated an honest, constructive conversation with her husband about her real feelings, wants, and needs. The couple then would have had the opportunity to do the kind of creative problem solving that can potentially result in a solution that satisfies both partners. For example, they might have agreed for Lilly to return to work part-time or to a budget that allowed some money for Lilly to spend on whatever she wanted.

Unfortunately, Lilly had bought into the "keep the peace at any cost" myth until she became miserable enough to end her marriage.

MARRIAGE MYTH #7: LOVE IS ALL YOU NEED

The Beatles notwithstanding, if you've read this far you know that for a good, lasting relationship, love is wonderful, but that the brain needs to be engaged to keep (what the Righteous Brothers called) "that loving feeling" alive and growing.

Singles who want to get married are often advised to make a

list of ten characteristics they are looking for in a mate. If you are married to someone who meets your basic requirements for a life partner, be grateful. But that is just the beginning. Love can grow or fade. If you want to keep loving feelings flowing, it is up to you. A simple way to keep your relationship on track is by holding weekly marriage meetings that cover all the basics.

MARRIAGE MYTH #8:
A WEEKLY MARRIAGE MEETING
CAN SAVE *ANY* MARRIAGE

It would be nice to be able to say that with the right tools and help, every committed relationship can become a lasting, successful one. But this is not true. Some relationships are doomed to fail because the couple got together for the wrong reasons. They did not recognize an unresolvable conflict that would become a deal breaker, like when one partner feels an absolute need to have children and the other is totally opposed to becoming a parent. When disagreement exists about a strongly held value, no number of marriage meetings or amount of couple therapy will assure a successful relationship.

A marriage can fail because at least one partner is not invested enough in the relationship to devote the energy it takes to make it succeed, which can include committing to individual or couple therapy or both.

Marriage partners who take their vows seriously know that marriage is a journey, not a destination. The long-term relationship you have always wanted is not an effortless happily-ever-after fairy tale come true but an ongoing process that requires regular proactive maintenance by both of you.

Because most of us are human, not saints, we are naturally selfish. Our challenge is to set a higher priority on the success of our relationship than on replaying less-than-healthy, entrenched patterns that may provide a familiar sense of comfort. Rather than entering into a win-lose power struggle with your partner, the two of you can each strive to respect the other's right — and your own — to have a different perspective on an issue. Only then can you journey toward mutual understanding and, in the process, find solutions that honor both your partner's and your own desires and needs.

Successful weekly marriage meetings can reduce or eliminate the need for therapy and counseling. However, the meetings alone are not a cure-all for every relationship. Some situations call out for assistance from a compassionate, skilled professional who can help you identify and resolve or manage issues that continue to fester.

About half the couples who attend my Marriage Meeting workshops continued to hold the meetings afterward. A follow-up survey showed that every one of these couples reported a happier, more loving relationship.

Knowledge Is Power

When you find yourself stewing about something that is at odds with your view of a good marriage, dig inside yourself to discover whether you are tuning in to fact or fiction. You may be listening to a marriage-myth channel. Once you clear up your thinking, you are on your way to the kind of marriage you really want — a happy, fulfilling one that lets each of you be who you really are, and with room to grow.

Marriage Meetings Can Set You Free

Effective marriage meetings will also help to free you from believing marriage myths. The structure and guidelines of the meetings foster healthy behaviors that reinforce realistic thinking.

For example, suppose you believe that love is all you need and there is no reason to invest energy in keeping your relationship good. But over time you've become unhappy. You feel overburdened with household chores and get little help from your partner. You are often too tired and resentful for sex and your spouse is upset about that.

Or some other unresolved issue has been causing you to feel distant. You used to believe that your love would see you through any challenges. You now take each other for granted. You can't remember the last time the two of you went on a date, and you wonder, Whatever happened to romance? You feel almost like strangers living under the same roof, leading parallel lives.

Now let's say that you and your partner decide to take a leap of faith. You agree to finish reading this book and then to hold at least six weekly marriage meetings. You even schedule your first meeting way in advance, realistically allowing for time to finish reading this book first.

After establishing a pattern of successful marriage meetings, you can expect to find yourself noticing more of what you appreciate about each other. You are likely to start paying more attention to each other in general. You begin having dates again, doing enjoyable activities that you both like, away from the house, the chores, and the kids.

If you think about it, you will probably realize that the initial attraction you felt for each other had faded because you forgot to nurture it with good times together and by continuing to appreciate each other's positive traits.

Are you holding on to one or more of the marriage myths described here? Habits are powerful. So don't be surprised if old thoughts surface. By holding effective marriage meetings, you will practice constructive ways of relating that will replace the less effective ones.

Part II

---·◆·---

Conducting *the* Four Parts *of a* Marriage Meeting

CHAPTER  3

Expressing Appreciation

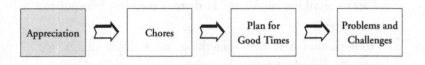

| Appreciation | ⇨ | Chores | ⇨ | Plan for Good Times | ⇨ | Problems and Challenges |

There is more hunger for love and appreciation in this world than for bread.

— MOTHER TERESA

Appreciation, the first part of a marriage meeting, helps you and your partner to reconnect by establishing a warm, positive climate. Of course, you do not need to wait for a meeting to give compliments, nor should you. But it is easy to start taking each other for granted. Marriage meetings reverse this tendency. They create a reservoir of good feelings and better communication skills.

HOW TO EXPRESS APPRECIATION

This is the basic order for conducting the Appreciation part of your weekly meeting:

1. One person goes first; for simplicity's sake, let's assume for now that this is you. (In practice, it usually works better to have the less verbal partner speak first; see page 40 for details.) You express appreciation now by saying everything you can think of that you specifically liked or admired about your partner during the past week. You can use the Appreciation Exercise on page 45 to prepare for this part of the meeting.

2. Your partner listens until you have finished.

3. When you have finished, you have the option to ask, "Did I leave anything out?" or "Is there something I forgot to mention?"

4. Your partner may add something, or multiple things, to your list for which he or she wants to be appreciated.

5. You agree with your partner, saying something like "Yes, I did appreciate that too."

6. Your partner says, "Thank you," when you have completed your list of appreciative comments.

7. Now it is time to reverse roles. Your partner becomes the speaker whose appreciative comments are directed to you, the new listener. The process I've just outlined is repeated with the new speaker and listener.

When you each tell the other what pleases you, this encourages you and your spouse to do these things more often. For example, let's suppose that when you arrive home, you want to hear "Hello" and maybe receive a hug and kiss. Usually you feel ignored, but about once a week you get the kind of greeting you value. If you say how happy you feel when this happens, it is likely to occur more often and you will both be glad about this.

Expressing gratitude builds intimacy, which promotes more appreciation. The more you focus on your partner's positive attributes and behaviors, the more often you will continue to notice them.

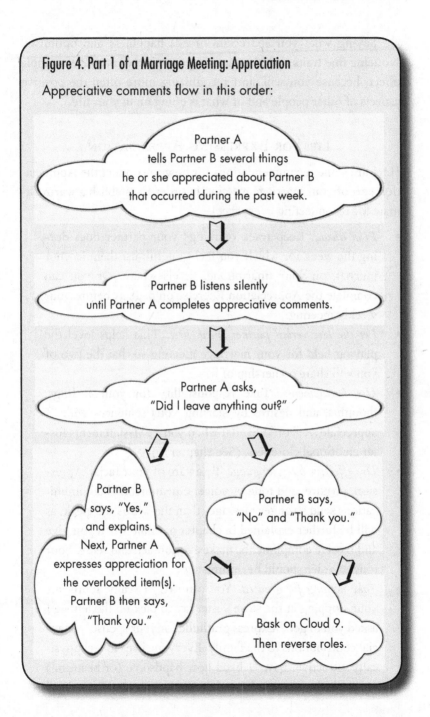

Figure 4. Part 1 of a Marriage Meeting: Appreciation

Appreciative comments flow in this order:

Partner A tells Partner B several things he or she appreciated about Partner B that occurred during the past week.

Partner B listens silently until Partner A completes appreciative comments.

Partner A asks, "Did I leave anything out?"

Partner B says, "Yes," and explains. Next, Partner A expresses appreciation for the overlooked item(s). Partner B then says, "Thank you."

Partner B says, "No" and "Thank you."

Bask on Cloud 9. Then reverse roles.

Saying what you appreciate breeds happiness and optimism. Noticing fine traits and behaviors in your partner produces a ripple effect, because you will start recognizing more often the positive aspects of other people and of what is going on in your life.

TIPS FOR EXPRESSING APPRECIATION

Here are some recommendations for how to conduct the Appreciation part of your marriage meeting in order to establish a warm climate for reconnecting every week.

- *Plan ahead.* Keep track of things your partner does during the week for which you feel grateful; list them in your journal, on your smartphone, or elsewhere. Or you can complete the Appreciation Exercise on page 45 before your weekly meeting.

- *Let the less verbal partner speak first.* This helps level the playing field for your marriage meeting so that the two of you will share ownership of it.

- *Use I-statements.* Take responsibility for your feelings, thoughts, and desires by starting your sentences with "I appreciate...," or "I liked it when you..." I-statements foster emotional closeness. (See chapter 7.)

- *Use effective body language.* Be aware of your facial expression, posture, and tone of voice. Our nonverbal communications send stronger messages than the words we speak, as will be further explained in chapter 9. Smile when you give and receive compliments, make eye contact, and relax. Your tone of voice should be optimistic.

- *Take nothing for granted.* You can say, "I really appreciate your stopping at the store yesterday to pick up the lettuce I asked you to get." Express gratitude for your spouse's financial contributions to the family. Everyone likes to feel physically attractive. Say, "I liked how handsome (or beautiful) you looked when you dressed up for the party last Saturday."

- *Compliment positive character traits.* In addition to expressing appreciation for specific behaviors, compliment your spouse for good personal qualities. Doing so produces a double dose of positive reinforcement. For example, "I appreciate *your empathy* in listening to me vent last night about my problem with a coworker. I value your *support*."

- *Ask yourself, "What else?"* Does he read a bedtime story to the children every night? Did you like her attentiveness at the party when she caught your eye from across the room and smiled? Did you appreciate his consideration in calling last night to say he would be home late?

- *Remember to listen silently.* While you are on the receiving end of appreciative comments, do not say a word until your partner has finished.

- *Be ready to add your two cents.* When your partner asks, "Have I left anything out?" you can say, "Do you appreciate the picnic lunch I packed for our outing to the lake last Sunday?" Your partner is likely to say, "Yes, I appreciate that too."

- *Stick with appreciation.* Do not even hint at disappointments or hurt feelings. Save them for part 4 of your marriage meeting, Problems and Challenges.

- *Avoid disguised you-statements.* These messages start with *I* but are actually accusations. "I appreciate that you *finally* remembered to take out the garbage on Wednesday night" is a disguised you-statement.

- *Be specific.* When and where did the appreciated behavior occur? What character trait did your partner show in the process?

After one false start, Janine and Fred quickly learned to be specific in expressing appreciation. When during their first try at a marriage meeting Janine told Fred, "I appreciate your thoughtfulness," his facial expression stayed bland. After I encouraged Janine to be more specific, she said, "I loved it when *you surprised me with the gorgeous long-stemmed red roses* on *Friday*, and I also appreciated your *thoughtfulness* in *putting them in the vase*." Fred brightened and said, "I don't know why it works to be specific, but it really does." When it was his turn to compliment Janine, he said, "I appreciated your *consideration* in *bringing me tea Wednesday evening* when my throat was sore." Janine lit up like a candle.

Occasionally, appreciation that lacks specificity is fine, as another couple learned. Marge said that during their first marriage meeting, "Steve told me, 'You hold it all together. You make it all happen.' It made me feel wonderful, even though it was global. I knew what he meant, that he appreciated everything I do as a wife, homemaker, and mother of our three children."

STRIVE FOR PROGRESS, NOT PERFECTION; APPRECIATE EACH OTHER'S EFFORTS

Can you recall the last time you complimented your spouse? What if compliments aren't flowing in your relationship? If that's true, expressing appreciation during your marriage meetings may feel awkward at first. Accept the feeling and do it anyway! Be patient and expect progress.

Emma had to learn this lesson. She complained that during their first marriage meeting the appreciative comments of her husband, Stuart, had been global. Nodding sheepishly, Stuart said, "I told her I appreciate how well she cleans the house. Since she cleans all the time I can't say anything special." I recommended to Emma that she give her husband more leeway as he experiments with new ways of communicating, and that she thank Stuart for his efforts.

She also can use the structure of the marriage meeting to help him learn to make appreciative comments that are more specific. When Stuart asks, after finishing expressing appreciation, "Have I left anything out?" Emma can say gently, "I wonder *what* you especially like about how I clean the house." That might remind him to say, "I like your *conscientiousness* in *using biodegradable cleaning products* and your *thoroughness* in *getting the dust out of all the corners.*"

When it's Emma's turn to give appreciation, she can show Stuart the kind of detailed appreciative comments she would like to hear from him by making sure to be specific in her compliments to him.

WHAT HOLDS US BACK
FROM EXPRESSING APPRECIATION?

Some people have trouble giving and receiving compliments. A few reasons for this:

Issues of self-worth. People who lack self-esteem find it difficult to accept appreciation. They don't believe they deserve it. They may withhold the giving of compliments out of fear that if their partner's self-image improves, he or she will leave the relationship.

Cultural considerations. People raised in cultures where accepting a compliment is viewed as boasting may feel uncomfortable when praised. Compliment such a person's haircut, and you can expect to hear about what's wrong with it.

Childhood influences. People whose parents did not compliment them while they were growing up may find it difficult to express and receive appreciative comments.

Difficulty allowing oneself to be vulnerable. Some people were raised in an environment where self-disclosure was risky. They may have been put down or punished for expressing their true feelings.

How Do You Feel When
Someone Gives You a Compliment?

When complimented, do you feel happy? Proud? Uncomfortable? Embarrassed? Thrilled? Do you like hearing it? If you find it hard to give and receive compliments, ask yourself why. Becoming aware of what might be getting in your way is the first step toward increasing your comfort with appreciation.

Can't Think of Anything to Appreciate?

Completing the Appreciation Exercise (see page 45) can help you come up with ideas before your meeting. But if you choose not to plan ahead, are miffed at your partner, or for some other reason are having difficulty expressing appreciation, find something positive to say anyway.

For example, you might start with "I appreciate that you are here meeting with me; it shows that you care about our relationship." Or "I like how you look in that shirt; the color brings out the blue in your eyes." Once you get started, you are likely to soon feel better about your spouse and come up with heartfelt compliments.

If you are feeling tempted to criticize your partner during the Appreciation part of your marriage meeting, exercise self-control and be patient. You can initiate a constructive discussion about a complaint during the fourth part of your marriage meeting, Problems and Challenges. Now is the time to reap the benefits of pure, undiluted, 100 percent appreciation.

Dos and Don'ts for Expressing Appreciation

- *Do* use I-statements.
- *Do* use effective body language.
- *Do* express appreciation for your partner's positive character traits.
- *Do* listen silently while receiving compliments, and thank your partner at the end.
- *Do* be specific.
- *Don't* omit the obvious.

- *Don't* interrupt during your partner's turn to express appreciation.
- *Don't* criticize. Every comment you make should be appreciative.
- *Don't* fall into the trap of thinking there is nothing to appreciate.

 APPRECIATION EXERCISE

List at least *five* specific things your partner did during the past week that you appreciate. Identify which positive character trait (such as demonstrating helpfulness, taking responsibility, showing thoughtfulness, and so on) your partner displayed when doing the behaviors you liked. For example:

- "I appreciate your kindness in listening when I griped about my job on Tuesday."
- "I like your consideration in turning off your phone during dinner every night this week."
- "I appreciate your thoughtfulness in putting gas in my car yesterday."
- "I appreciate your tender lovemaking Saturday night."

Now it's your turn. Begin sentences in your journal or on a separate sheet of paper as shown in the following list. Complete each sentence in a way that expresses your appreciation of your spouse.

1. I appreciate...
2. I appreciate...
3. I like(d)...
4. I appreciate...
5. I appreciate...

CHAPTER  4

Coordinating Chores

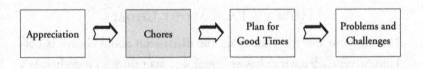

| Appreciation | ⇨ | Chores | ⇨ | Plan for Good Times | ⇨ | Problems and Challenges |

After enlightenment, the laundry.

— JOSH BILLINGS

What do you think when you hear the word *chores?* Nobody is looking for more to do in a busy life. But if we want to live in a supportive milieu, we need to find ways to take care of chores while still taking care of ourselves.

Think of chores as simple tasks that produce a harmonious environment that is worth investing energy into maintaining. Taking care of a home is like running a small business. To keep it thriving, many jobs need to be handled on a regular basis.

The Chores part of a marriage meeting proceeds like a business meeting. No matter how great a relationship you already have, you can probably gain better teamwork. Not to mention the fringe benefits: Sweeping, dishwashing, and doing laundry may not seem to have any connection to a couple's level of romance and intimacy and their sex life. In fact, several studies report the opposite to be true — that couples who share household tasks have sex more often than those in which one partner slacks off in the chores arena. A husband in one of these studies said his wife enjoys flowers or a candlelit restaurant dinner, "but if he wants to be sure of a romantic evening, he goes for the vacuum cleaner."[1]

Conduct the Chores part of your marriage meeting as described in the following discussion, and your home may not be the only thing that glows.

How to Talk about Chores

During your marriage meeting, the discussion about chores is collaborative; each partner has an equal say. Set priorities together. It's easy to feel overwhelmed by a long to-do list. Don't let this happen to you. When useful to do so, break down big jobs into smaller parts.

Begin talking about chores with each of you saying what tasks you view as urgent and which as less pressing. Either partner can speak first, and you can take turns saying what each of you thinks. But if one of you is more task-minded than the other, it is fine for that person to initiate most of the discussions. Here's how to talk about chores:

1. You and your partner each say what chores are on your to-do list.
2. Together, decide which tasks need to get handled within the next week and which can wait.
3. Agree on who will do each task or will arrange for someone else (e.g., a family member, cleaning service, or plumber) to do it. Ideally, decide who does what task based on individual schedules, abilities, and interests.
4. Set time lines for some future tasks and put others on hold, by mutual agreement.

5. Give progress reports on the status of chores you agreed to do (or delegate) in previous meetings. Report on any chore you did not finish by the agreed-upon time.

If any discussion during the Chores part of your marriage meeting becomes emotionally charged, move it to part 4 of the marriage meeting, Problems and Challenges.

Also, realize that once in a while a situation may arise that calls for you to change a priority, revise a time line, or renegotiate who

---

Figure 5. Part 2 of a Marriage Meeting: Chores

❏ 1. Each partner mentions chores on his or her to-do list.

❏ 2. Partners agree on which chores to do or begin this week and which can wait.

❏ 3. Partners agree on who will handle or delegate each chore to be done during the coming week.

❏ 4. Partners set time lines for some future projects and put others on hold.

❏ 5. Each partner reports on progress regarding tasks discussed in previous meetings.

Notes:
- If a discussion about a chore becomes emotionally charged, move that topic to part 4 of the meeting, Problems and Challenges.
- When the situation calls for it, be willing to revise priorities, time lines, and responsibilities.

will be responsible for a task. Of course, you will want to be flexible at such times, by agreeing to revise a prior agreement in a manner that suits both of you.

 Chores — Exercise 1

Before you and your partner talk about chores in your marriage meeting, ask yourself these questions and write the answers in your notebook:

- Is your to-do list overwhelming?
- What chores do each of you handle routinely?
- Are you satisfied with how you and your partner decide who does what?
- Are you unhappy about how your spouse handles a chore?
- What chores are being delegated to children at home or to other people?
- Who is responsible for supervising the participation of others in handling chores?
- Are your discussions about chores stressful?

By answering these questions honestly, you learn about the

1. areas in which you and your spouse are functioning well as a team,
2. areas in which you would like teamwork to improve, and
3. chores that you may want to prioritize, postpone handling, or delegate to others.

Reflecting on your answers will prepare you to bring up your concerns during the Chores part of your marriage

---

meeting. You may decide to ask your partner to put away clean laundry sooner, vacuum more regularly, or empty the garbage before it overflows. You may want to discuss how to get chores done for which no one is currently responsible, such as by delegating jobs to other members of the household.

Plan Ahead to Decide on Chores to Discuss

The value of making lists has been proven.[2] Before your first meeting, if you list all the tasks necessary to do in order for your household to run smoothly — such as food shopping, cooking, lawn maintenance, emptying the garbage, paying bills, and so on — you will have taken the first step toward handling them more efficiently. Next to each job, note which person is currently doing it. As part of the meeting, you can decide together who will take care of the ones that no one is currently doing.

During a marriage meeting, you need not talk about chores for which you have already established a comfortable routine. For example, if one of you always cooks dinner and the other cleans up afterward, and both of you are happy with this arrangement, there is no reason to bring up the subject during Chores.

In advance of your weekly meeting, you may want to make a list of pressing tasks to mention, or you can complete Chores — Exercise 2 on page 60.

Discuss Chores Respectfully

In a Marriage Meeting workshop, I demonstrated how to talk about a chore respectfully. I played the role of the wife of a participant who had come by himself. In a casual tone, I said, "The leaky faucet in the bathroom needs to be fixed. It looks like we need a plumber. Should I call one, or do you want to set up the appointment?"

"Wow!" said one woman. Others looked surprised and impressed. A direct question asked respectfully was a new option for many who observed our interaction.

Some spouses demand that their partner do a chore, blurting out, "You *need* to call the plumber" or "Do it tomorrow." The other might think, or say through clenched teeth, "Why always me? Why don't you do it for a change?"

A passive partner is less likely to argue. This sort of person, when feeling bossed around by his or her spouse regarding a chore, might say okay and then express resentment less directly, such as by forgetting to do the task, withdrawing from the "demanding" spouse, or losing interest in sex.

Couples who follow the guidelines in this chapter and in chapters 7, 8, and 9 will accomplish their to-do list priorities and strengthen their partnership.

Strive for a spirit of give-and-take in which both of you take on a reasonable share of chores. Don't adopt an even-steven mentality. Set limits regarding how much you are willing to take on. Allow time to relax; everyone needs enough downtime to lead a balanced life. Let go of perfectionism when it interferes with enjoying life. Good enough is usually fine.

When the Situation Calls for It, Revise Priorities and Time Lines

The day after Dina and Jason had decided to replace their kitchen flooring, their roof started leaking. So they agreed it made sense to take care of the roof first. Another time, after Jason agreed to start organizing receipts for income tax preparation on Monday, he was asked to work overtime that day. So they agreed he would organize the tax-related documents on Tuesday instead.

Deciding Who Does What

Meals need to be prepared. A child needs a ride to soccer practice. Receipts need to get organized in preparation for calculating income tax. The roof needs to be repaired.

Either partner may volunteer to handle any chore. Do not assign your partner a job to do or assume that he or she will do it. We all want to feel autonomous. It is fine to ask about a partner's availability or willingness. But realize that no one wants to be told what to do or be taken for granted.

Partners should negotiate who will do a task neither wants to do. They may decide to share the job, take turns doing it, or delegate it to someone else. For example, sharing could mean that one cooks dinner and the other makes a salad to eat with it. Taking turns could mean that on some days the wife prepares the whole meal and on other days the husband does. Delegating can mean that a teenage child is given the responsibility of preparing the meal at certain times.

Ideally, whoever has the skill, time, ability, and inclination to do a particular task offers to do it. The partner who is good with numbers is the likely one to balance the checkbook(s) and pay the bills. The physically stronger partner does the heavy lifting.

Delegate Tasks to Children and Others When Appropriate

Avoid falling into a parent-as-servant role, which can put stress on a marriage and prevents children from maturing into responsible adults. A child old enough to carry a toy can bring napkins to the table. Obviously, older ones can do much more.

By giving your children age-appropriate responsibilities, everyone gains. Your load gets lightened while you build good character traits and self-esteem in your children. Family harmony and teamwork increase.

You may decide to hire outside help, such as a housecleaning or gardening service. Be realistic about how much you and other family members can do. Accepting limitations is healthy. If you can swing it financially, it is well worth paying someone to do an important job that otherwise will not receive the needed attention. In some situations you may be able to avoid the expense of getting some work done by exchanging services with a friend.

TRY A FRESH APPROACH

If you are annoyed about a chore not getting done, be resourceful in seeking solutions. For example, if dust buildup keeps bothering you, consider these possibilities:

- Get outside help, such as by hiring a housecleaner.
- Agree to eliminate a lower-priority chore to free up time to vacuum and dust.
- Be willing to lower your standards. The *perfect* is the enemy of the *good*.
- Assign the chore to another family member, such as a teenager.

Is reducing clutter important to you? By communicating your concern to your spouse during the Chores part of your meeting, you will be taking the first step toward arriving at a solution mutually. Use I-statements (see chapter 7) and a respectful tone. If you sense you are not being heard, or if the topic feels emotionally charged, move this discussion to part 4 of your marriage meeting, Problems and Challenges, and use the recommended communication techniques that appear in chapters 7, 8, and 9.

CHANGING A ROUTINE

Like most of us, Sue and her husband, Harry, are creatures of habit. She cooks; he cleans up afterward. It's been this way since they married eight years ago. For a change of pace, Sue now wants a break one night a week from cooking dinner. Because Harry is used to their routine, Sue expects him to resist her suggestion that he start cooking on Sunday nights.

Before reading about how Sue handled the matter, think about how you might approach a similar situation. How do you currently go about trying to change or clarify who does what chore?

Would you want to mention your concern while your partner is reading, watching television, driving, or otherwise occupied? By bringing up the topic during your marriage meeting, you will increase the likelihood of a productive discussion.

This is what Sue does, now that she and Harry have already held a series of effective marriage meetings. She brings up her idea during the Chores part of their next marriage meeting. Sue begins the conversation with an I-statement, telling her husband, "I've been thinking I'd like to have a break from cooking once a week. I'd love eating a home-cooked meal that I haven't had to prepare."

Harry squirms a bit and says, "You mean you want me to, uh… cook?"

Sue treads carefully. Again, she uses an I-statement. "I'd love for you to cook the main meal once a week, maybe on Sundays. I can do the cleanup afterward."

Harry says quietly, not meeting her eyes, "Maybe once in a while."

Sue views this as negotiating. She wants more than he just offered. Understanding that her husband is reluctant, she softens her request. Keeping her tone light and her expression cheerful, she asks, "How about trying out cooking one meal on the next two Sundays? It could be brunch or dinner."

"Maybe…" He's not saying yes, but he's not ruling out the idea either. He can probably handle two meals, he thinks.

Sue sweetens the offer by making it even simpler for him: "This

Sunday, if you'd rather not make the whole meal, you can just heat up leftovers you find in the fridge. I'd be okay with that."

Harry understands that she is asking for very little now and agrees to prepare dinner on the next two Sundays.

Do you see how Sue and Harry succeeded in changing a routine? Sue began by saying what she would most like to have happen: for her husband to cook dinner once a week. She noticed her husband's reluctance and respected his feelings. Each time that she softened her request and he resisted, she suggested an easier way for him to comply, until she made an offer that was acceptable to him.

Sue will make sure to compliment Harry for the great meal he has prepared on Sunday and will do so again during the Appreciation part of their next marriage meeting.

When Complications Arise

Sue and Harry spoke to each other respectfully. If you think the conversation is likely to become more complicated or emotionally charged than in their example, introduce your request during the fourth part of your marriage meeting, Problems and Challenges.

Wendy and Zack, whose story appears in chapter 13, illustrate how a discussion about a chore can flare into a conflict. During the Chores part of a marriage meeting, held in my office, Zack told Wendy, "You're disgusting. You went to sleep the other night leaving your dirty dishes on the kitchen table. You're a slob. And when's the last time you vacuumed? I'm sick of seeing kitty litter on the carpet. Tell your psychiatrist to give you some pills to make you see the mess you leave behind you. I can't live in a pigsty."

Wendy said, holding back tears, "I'm sorry, but I'm so tired after standing on my feet all day at work —"

Zack and Wendy were talking about something much bigger than a chore. It is true that Zack had been upset with her for a long time for what he considered her slipshod housekeeping style. But subconsciously he thought, "If she really cared about me, she would pick up after herself." And she thought but didn't say, "He doesn't love me, or he wouldn't be so mean."

This couple's provocative criticism, name-calling, and hurt feelings indicated that this topic was too emotionally charged for them to discuss rationally during Chores. It should have been moved to the Problems and Challenges part of their marriage meeting. Obviously, Zack and Wendy will also need to learn to use positive communication skills in order to hold a constructive discussion.

In a later couple session during which Zack and Wendy tried holding a marriage meeting, they were able to communicate respectfully and follow the agenda. When it was time for Problems and Challenges, I encouraged them to address their different housekeeping standards respectfully, which they were able to do. They arrived at a mutually acceptable solution by agreeing to hire a cleaning service.

Keep Agreements, Renegotiate as Necessary, and Build Trust

Ideally, both partners will keep agreements. Doing so builds trust. You can expect that at least occasionally an agreement will not be kept, because no one is perfect. If one of you has not completed a chore by an agreed-upon time, don't waste energy by blaming yourself or your spouse. Instead, say why you did not complete the task. Don't wait for your partner to notice that the item wasn't purchased at the hardware store or the lawn wasn't mowed. Provide your own explanation during your progress report at a marriage meeting, or sooner, then choose a realistic date for completing the task.

A partner who wants to know the status of a chore should ask about it during the Chores part of the meeting. If the task has not been completed when expected, agree on a new time by which it will be done. Move that job to the top of your to-do list and follow up on it at your next marriage meeting. The discussion should be respectful. Again, if an issue becomes heated, emotional, or too complicated to resolve quickly, the topic of concern should be moved to Problems and Challenges.

COUPLES AND MONEY

If you and your partner have established a routine for dealing with money, then brief reports and conversations about spending, saving, and investing money belong in Chores. For example, Betty might suggest to Joe that they move their savings to a bank that pays more interest. One of you might want to mention a large expense coming up, such as a property tax, a security deposit on a rental home, or an income tax that needs to be paid, and to discuss what source the money will come from.

Conflicts about who will pay for which expenses, how much discretionary spending each partner gets to do, or some other sensitive money matter should be discussed during the Problems and Challenges part of your marriage meeting.

There are no rules for how couples should deal with money. The topic is often emotionally charged because of what money symbolizes. For many people, it represents security, love, freedom, or power. Several fine books on the subject of couples and money are available. If an unresolved money conflict is gnawing away at your relationship, consult with a trusted friend, a financial or other counselor, or a psychotherapist who can help you address your concerns constructively.

APPRECIATE A SPOUSE'S EFFORTS

Partners need to know that their efforts in doing chores are appreciated, even when the results are less than perfect. The pot he washed may have a bit of food residue in it. She may have forgotten to vacuum up a few crumbs. A marriage is happier when partners accept each other's imperfections.

Enjoy the Teamwork

To manage chores in ways that work for both of you, first tell each other what is important to you, using I-statements and a respectful tone. Listen to your partner sensitively. Avoid a fifty-fifty mentality, which can lead to nitpicking, but do seek relief when one of you feels like your load has gotten too heavy. In order to keep yourselves emotionally and physically well, it is important to agree that you will try to accomplish no more than is realistic for either of you and to respect each other's limits. Allow the process of changing any of your routines to happen gradually. Experiment until you find out what is best for you as individuals and for your relationship.

Follow these guidelines and your love will grow. Mutual appreciation, trust, and respect flourish as each of you recognizes the other's contributions. It's no wonder that couples who share chores also have more sex. Go team!

DOS AND DON'TS FOR THE
CHORES PART OF A MARRIAGE MEETING

- *Do* list chores and agree on who is responsible for doing each one.
- *Do* set time lines for when each chore is to be completed.
- *Do* set priories *together*.
- *Do* put some chores on hold to make time for higher priorities.
- *Do* appreciate each other's efforts and accomplishments.
- *Do* give and ask for progress reports regarding previously

agreed-upon chores that have or have not yet been completed.

- *Don't* fret about a chore that should have been done. Move it to the top of the to-do list.
- *Don't* criticize how a partner handles a chore.
- *Don't* waste energy by blaming your partner or yourself for what hasn't been done.
- *Don't* allow arguing during this "business" part of the meeting.

 CHORES — EXERCISE 2

You can prepare in advance for the Chores part of your marriage meeting by writing your answers to the following questions in your journal or elsewhere:

- What tasks would you like to see accomplished within the coming week? Examples: "Call repair person to fix dishwasher by Thursday." "Buy curtains for bedroom within a week." After completing your chore list, indicate which one has top priority, and so on. Then note for which task(s) you are willing to be responsible.
- What future tasks do you want to mention, discuss, or set time lines for?
- For which projects would you like to give your partner a progress report, and for which ones would you like to receive a report?

Planning for Good Times

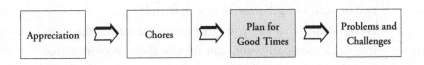

| Appreciation | ⇨ | Chores | ⇨ | Plan for Good Times | ⇨ | Problems and Challenges |

Enjoyable activities add juice to all your relationships; they recharge your batteries. By going out on dates with your spouse, you rekindle the spark that first attracted you. During part 3 of your meeting, Plan for Good Times, you schedule dates for the two of you. You also schedule family outings, enjoyable activities you do on your own, and get-togethers with others.

How to Plan for Good Times

Here's what you will plan:

- A date for just you and your partner during the coming week.
- At least one individual self-nurturing activity you will do within a week.
- Family outings, if children are in the home and available.
- Possible get-togethers with extended family members or friends.
- Vacations for yourselves and for your family.

As usual, use positive communication skills during your discussion, especially I-statements, as described in chapter 7; and active listening and brainstorming for solutions, both of which are explained in chapter 9.

The procedure to follow in this part of your marriage meeting is simple:

1. First, one or both of you suggests possible activities for your weekly date together. You may also want to mention self-nurturing activities you plan to do on your own, and to offer ideas for family outings and vacations, getaways for just the two of you, and get-togethers with friends.
2. Next, decide what you will do on your date during the coming week. Similarly, you can decide about activities that include other people and about vacations.
3. Then, schedule a day and time for your date. You may also want to schedule other activities, vacations, and so on.

Some couples who attend a marriage meeting workshop seem stumped when it comes to arranging a date. Their lives have been focused on work, money, children, and projects for so long that they have forgotten about having fun together.

Do you remember when the two of you fell in love? It wasn't while vacuuming, doing laundry, or making a mortgage payment, was it? More likely, you first met in a pleasant setting. You were relaxed. You felt an attraction. Then you went out on dates. *Out* is the key word. You went out. You escaped from daily responsibilities and to-do lists. You felt happy and excited. Love blossomed. You got married.

Sometime later you may have begun to wonder, "What happened to romance?" Although the initial ecstasy lessens as real life sets in, you needn't live as platonic roommates. You *can* fall in love with your spouse again and again.

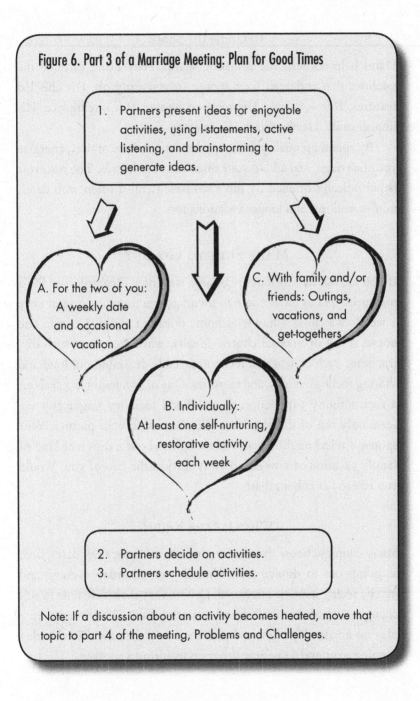

Figure 6. Part 3 of a Marriage Meeting: Plan for Good Times

1. Partners present ideas for enjoyable activities, using I-statements, active listening, and brainstorming to generate ideas.

A. For the two of you: A weekly date and occasional vacation

B. Individually: At least one self-nurturing, restorative activity each week

C. With family and/or friends: Outings, vacations, and get-togethers

2. Partners decide on activities.
3. Partners schedule activities.

Note: If a discussion about an activity becomes heated, move that topic to part 4 of the meeting, Problems and Challenges.

Rekindle the Spark

Dates help rekindle the romantic spark. They bring to mind the qualities that endeared your spouse to you early on. His chiseled features. Her soft eyes. His sense of humor. Her intelligence. His impish smile. Her kindness. His sweetness.

By spending quality time together, you will reconnect, energize your marriage, and add to your reservoir of goodwill. The reservoir is periodically drained by life's stresses. Refill it often with dates, mini-vacations, and longer vacations too.

MAKE SURE TO GO *OUT*

If you are not having dates regularly, start now. Regardless of life's pressures, *and* as an antidote to them, go out together at least once a week. Watching a movie at home does not count. Go *out*. The house is full of undone chores. Ideally, while free from such distractions, each of you will feel comfortable dreaming out loud and sharing feelings, hopes, and fantasies. One of you might laugh about a recent funny experience. A childhood memory might pop up, seemingly out of the blue, that you share with your partner. Your spouse's mind might wander to thoughts about a different kind of family vacation or a weekend away for just the two of you. Would you like to hear about that?

When Is Date Night?

Many couples choose the same night each week for their dates, such as going out to dinner each Thursday or Saturday evening and maybe seeing a movie afterward. Others vary their date time to suit changing schedules or to attend a special event. They might see a play on a Saturday night and plan their next date for a Wednesday evening to attend a onetime program featuring a speaker.

Adopting a Positive Dating Attitude

Make each date a special occasion. Dress up. Be positive, polite, and attentive to your partner. When other people see you looking wonderful, your spouse will view you with new eyes and vice versa. Enjoy the view. Compliment each other for looking great.

The two of you want to reconnect as lovers, right? An evening out with others is fine now and then but does not count as a date.

If you go out to a movie or performance during which talking is discouraged, converse before and after it. Take a walk, go to a coffee shop, or be creative in finding another way to hang out together as a couple.

You may want to talk a lot or a little. Silence *can* be golden. Much communication happens nonverbally, with a smile, a hug, a thoughtful gesture, or by looking into each other's eyes. Leave your troubles at home. This is the time to enjoy yourselves.

DEALING WITH EXCUSES

Plan activities you both enjoy. If money is an issue, don't let it get in the way. Couples who stop dating after being married for a while may protest, "We can't afford to go out." They cite the cost of dinner at an upscale restaurant or high-priced concert or play. Other excuses are "We're too busy" and "There's no one to watch our children."

None of these reasons hold water. In fact, if you are using any of these excuses, you are draining water from your reservoir of goodwill. Refill the reservoir.

Overcoming Money Excuses

If money's tight, be a cheap date! Here are suggestions for low-cost or no-cost dates:

- Pack a picnic from your fridge and pantry. Take it to a scenic area. You can dress up your outing with a tablecloth.
- Attend a free talk by an author at a library, at a bookstore, or on a college campus.
- Take a long scenic walk, hike, or bike ride.
- Drive to a nice spot for stargazing.
- Hang out at a cozy café where you can nurse a cup of your favorite drink.
- Splurge on a sandwich at the café.
- See a play at a community theater or on a college campus.
- Go to a beach.
- People-watch at an interesting location.
- Go window-shopping.

What other free or low-cost activities might you and your partner enjoy?

My thinking about couples who say they are too busy to go out on a date together is that they need to rethink their priorities. Ask yourself these questions: "Do I value an intimate connection with my partner?" and "Isn't it possible to delegate, postpone, or eliminate at least one or two activities in order to free up time to fall in love again with him or her?"

Sometimes parents say that they cannot go out on dates because there is no one to take care of their children. But almost anyone who is willing to be resourceful can arrange for child care. It's a matter of priorities. You will realize the value of taking time for yourselves to go out as a couple when you do so.

Here are a few ideas for people who find it difficult to arrange for child care:

- Hire a responsible teenager to sit. Obtain and check references.
- To get names of potential sitters, contact other parents or a local Red Cross agency, which may have a training program

for babysitters in your area, or a nearby high school that may have a register of sitters.

- Join or start a babysitting co-op.
- Trade babysitting services with friends.

Be flexible about where the babysitting will occur. One New Year's Eve my husband and I wanted to go out but weren't able to find a sitter for our child. A friend offered to take care of him in her home, and we accepted. Our son had a great time playing with her boys. He was asleep when we picked him up around midnight.

WHAT IF YOU'VE GOTTEN OUT OF THE FUN GROOVE?

For some couples it has been so long since they dated that they seem to have forgotten how. The solution is to brainstorm for fun activities. Ask yourself, "What activities did we like doing with each other before marriage? What did I love doing as a child?" Together, dream about things you would like to do and places you would like to go. Each of you should make your own list, using "Plan for Good Times — Exercise 1" as a guide.

 PLAN FOR GOOD TIMES — EXERCISE 1

Some husbands and wives say it's been so long since they've gone out together or individually just to enjoy themselves, they've forgotten how. If this sounds like you, this exercise can help. In your journal or elsewhere, follow these steps, making a chart similar to the example below.

List at least ten activities you've enjoyed before or think that you would like to do now. Include things you would like to do with your partner, as well as activities you would enjoy doing on your own. Some examples to help you get started include: go to the beach, walk in the woods, go dancing, attend a concert, take a bubble bath, receive a back massage, take a yoga class, ski, ice skate, snowboard, or spend a week on a tropical island.

Write how long it's been since you've done each one.

Indicate whether each can be done alone or requires another person. (In the third column of the chart, you can write *A* if the activity is done *alone*, *P* if it is done with a *partner*.)

Indicate whether each is free or costs money.

Identify when you would like to schedule each activity or a step you can take to make it happen.

Here is an example of how to begin this exercise.

Activity	Last Time Done	A or P	$ or Free	Action Step/ Schedule
1. Kayaking (rent)	A month ago	A, P	$	This Sunday
2. Hiking	Don't remember	A, P	Free	Set a date with spouse
3. Read a novel	Two months ago	A	Free	Go to library on Friday
4. See a play	Six months ago	A, P	$	A week from Sunday

Again, if you're feeling challenged to come up with ideas, think back to how you and your spouse enjoyed spending time together while dating. Recall what you used to do for fun as a child and teenager. Or you can do an internet search for "list of pleasurable activities" for more possibilities.

Share your completed lists with each other. By comparing lists, you will see which interests you share and identify activities for the two of you to do together, as well as those to do on your own or with someone else. Then plan mutually enjoyable dates. This process will help get you back on the recreation track. The tragically high divorce rates result partly from couples' investing too much energy elsewhere while neglecting their relationship. When that happens, partners become estranged emotionally and physically.

So do schedule dates and keep them. These are precious times. They build trust, which is a must for intimacy. Barring illness, accident, or family emergency, keep your date as a sacred occasion.

If Necessary, Dig Deeper

Some husbands and wives who have stopped dating each other may fear that if they start again they will have nothing to talk about, or worse, that their partner will criticize them. Agree not to allow this to happen. Make each date a good experience for both of you. Decide to keep your focus positive. You can bring up sensitive issues during your marriage meetings once you have established a series of successful meetings (or in a therapy session, if necessary).

If you've read this far and are still finding reasons not to go out together, determine what the real issue is, either by yourselves or with help from a skilled therapist, counselor, or wise friend. Most of us find time to do what we want to do, even with busy schedules.

Reconnecting

By going on a date with your spouse every week, you will keep the romantic spark glowing. You will look forward to these times with excitement. Make them happy events for both of you. Your intimacy and love for each other will flourish.

PLANNING DATES WITH YOURSELF

Julia Cameron, author of *The Artist's Way,* encourages all of us, not just artists, to schedule a weekly "artist date."[1] She advises us to devote a block of time, about two hours at least once a week, to being *alone* while engaging in a self-nurturing activity. Our true, uncensored thoughts and feelings emerge spontaneously during such periods. Ideas arise for creative ways to address challenges we may be experiencing in marriage or elsewhere. By doing pleasurable activities on your own, you connect to your essence and feel more alive. Your revitalized self will positively affect your marriage and your other relationships and activities.

Most likely your partner was initially attracted by your vibrancy. You were happy and confident because you took good care of yourself. With all the pressures of married and family life, it's easy to forget to nurture ourselves. We may stop doing things that used to energize us, or do them less often. When this happens, we may lose our sense of having a separate, unique identity.

What If You Feel Guilty Taking Time for Yourself?

Do you feel guilty about taking time for yourself? If yes, you are not alone, and you are still a good person. If you weren't a good person, you wouldn't be caring enough to read this book, would you? So accept the feeling, and then do it anyway! Take time for yourself.

We do not need to be controlled by our feelings. Instead, put your brain in charge. Take a tip from marriage and relationship educator Ellen Kreidman, who explained the importance of filling up your "love cup" via self-nurture.[2] If you neglect to take care of yourself, your relationships with yourself, your partner, and others will suffer. If you do not fill up your love cup regularly, you will be unhappy. This feeling might show up as depression, anger, loss of interest in sex, thoughts of divorce, or as an addictive syndrome, such as alcoholism, overeating, drug use, or smoking.

The joie de vivre you gain from indulging in a good time on your own creates a ripple effect, energizing not just yourself but also your partner, family members, and others. People will be drawn to your vitality. You will handle your responsibilities with more ease. Everything flows more smoothly for a happy person.

If you're still feeling guilty about being nice to yourself, remember: no one likes being around a martyr. Do not become one. The expression "When Mom's happy, everyone's happy" is true not just for mothers but also for both spouses. Refill your love cup often. If you need to jump-start yourself in order to think of fun activities you can do alone, do an internet search for "list of pleasurable activities" to see hundreds of possibilities. See which activities appeal to you. Then you can schedule a time to refill your love cup.

Togetherness —Too Much of a Good Thing?

Some people think it is necessary to give up separate interests after marriage. Nothing could be further from the truth. By depriving yourself of individual, self-nurturing activities, you are likely to start feeling uneasy. Your self-esteem will drop. You may resent your partner.

If you value romance, emotional intimacy, and a healthy sex life, do not insist on the kind of "togetherness" that sucks the vitality out of you. Make sure to engage in enjoyable, restorative activities on your own and with others.

FAMILY OUTINGS

Family outings foster bonding, goodwill, and cooperation. Going somewhere as a family for a few hours, a day, a weekend, or longer, increases harmony at home.

Most likely, you will find it easy to arrange for activities everyone will enjoy. When your children are very young, you will make the decisions. Older children are likely to want to have a say in planning family outings and trips, so encourage them to share their ideas.

Accommodating Different Interests

Occasions may arise when different preferences are expressed and it seems hard for everyone to agree on what to do and where to go. This actually happened in one of our family meetings some time ago, when we were planning a short vacation. We were holding these as well as marriage meetings, using the same four-part agenda.

My husband and our son wanted to go camping. I did not. Don't get me wrong. I love going to sleep under a sky full of shining stars, waking up in a tent surrounded by huge evergreen trees, smelling the fresh, forest scents and the aroma of breakfast cooking outside. But I don't sleep well on the ground or a flimsy cot, so I'm not much fun to be with the next morning.

Brainstorming for a Family Vacation Solution

We moved the trip-planning issue to Problems and Challenges. Each of us said what activities we would like to do wherever we went. I wrote down each suggestion. My husband and son both mentioned camping. I suggested kayaking and river rafting. My husband said he'd like to visit a Wild West ghost town and our son agreed. I wanted to spend at least an hour or two by the lake. My son said he would rather hike. Once we had the list, we looked it over to see what we could all agree on. Everyone liked kayaking and river rafting. My husband and son were willing to give up the camping idea. I was not eager to traipse around a ghost town, but in a spirit of give-and-take I agreed to it. I realized that I could either relax at the lake while the two of them hiked or join them. We decided to stay in the Lake Tahoe area because it was possible to do everything we were interested in there. We made plans accordingly and had a wonderful time.

In case you are wondering, the guys did get to go camping, but on a different trip, with another dad and his two sons. I stayed home. A good time was had by all.

GOOD TIMES RECHARGE EVERYONE'S BATTERIES

It is easy to get bogged down dealing with to-do lists and life's challenges. Don't try to run on empty. We all need breaks to keep functioning well. Making time for fun will spice up your marital relationship, increase family harmony, and buoy you up for confidently handling whatever comes your way.

Dos and Don'ts for Planning for Good Times

- *Do* take time to think of enjoyable activities.
- *Do* plan for good times alone, as a couple, and as a family.
- *Do* make "artist's dates" for yourself.
- *Do* encourage your spouse to engage individually in self-nurturing activities.
- *Don't* fall into the martyr trap. Investing in time for yourself reaps benefits for all.
- *Don't* forget to plan vacations — as a couple, as a family, and perhaps also one for just yourself.

Plan for Good Times — Exercise 2

You can prepare for your marriage meeting by listing in your journal or elsewhere the answers to these questions:

1. What ideas do you have for enjoyable activities during the next week?
   a. As a couple
   b. Individually
   c. With family and/or with friends
2. What ideas do you have for vacations as a couple, as a family, and possibly individually?

Addressing Problems and Challenges

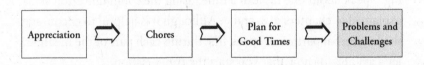

| Appreciation | ⇒ | Chores | ⇒ | Plan for Good Times | ⇒ | Problems and Challenges |

Marriage is an alliance entered into by a man who can't sleep with the
window shut, and a woman who can't sleep with the window open.

— GEORGE BERNARD SHAW

Problems and Challenges is the last part of the marriage meeting for
a good reason. Picture yourself having just completed the first three
parts of the meeting. You feel appreciated, you know the chores will
get done, and you're looking forward to a fun date the two of you
have just planned. Of course you're in a good mood.

Yes, you still have concerns. Who doesn't? But now you feel
"We're in this together" and "We can handle this." You are ready
to face challenges as a team, to come up with solutions that work
for both of you. As you resolve issues, you gain a serene sense of
closure. You have cleaned up mental clutter that was weighing
you down. Also, you look forward to completing your meeting by

75

adding frosting to the cake with an upbeat ending, which will be explained shortly.

HOW TO DISCUSS PROBLEMS AND CHALLENGES

Here's how to hold the Problems and Challenges part of your marriage meeting: Either of you can bring up any issue. Select just one or two concerns to discuss at each meeting, three at the most, so you can stay focused and constructive. Do not overwhelm yourself by bringing a laundry list of subjects to discuss at a single meeting. Speak about one topic at a time, using the communication skills explained in chapters 7, 8, and 9. Although it is helpful to encourage the less verbal partner to speak first during each part of the meeting, let's assume for now that you start the conversation.

1. You introduce a concern. Use I-statements (see chapter 7) to create a respectful tone. Bring up only easy-to-resolve challenges during your first four to six meetings. Doing so will build trust and confidence in both of you that you can use later in dealing with harder-to-resolve ones.

2. Your partner listens until you have finished saying what is on your mind.

3. Once you feel understood by your partner, he or she responds, also using I-statements. You listen attentively.

4. Continue the discussion, remembering to use positive communication skills until both of you feel heard and understood.

5. Possible results from the exchange:
   a. Partners arrive at an agreement for how to handle the concern.
   b. Partners lack agreement and decide to continue the discussion at a future meeting.
   c. Partners accept a problem as one that is not resolvable,

such as a trait in a spouse that is unlikely to change, but with which they can learn to live.

    d. Partners discover over time that they are not able to resolve a conflict, and that it is driving a wedge between them. In that case, they should seek help from a therapist, marriage counselor, or other qualified person.

6. If time permits, after discussing the first issue, either of you can bring up another one, using the sequence described here.

7. When you have finished the Problems and Challenges part of your marriage meeting, end it on a positive note. Thank each other for participating. Show your appreciation with a handshake or hug, or in any way that makes you happy.

Add an Upbeat Ending to Your Marriage Meeting

After concluding your marriage meeting, do an activity you enjoy. You might decide to share a dessert together. Or you may want some separate, alone time. Do what fits for each of you.

KEEPING SMALL ANNOYANCES FROM GETTING BIG

What causes the breakup of many relationships are little things that are allowed to get big. Here is a simple example that shows how a couple can deal effectively with a minor, seemingly trivial annoyance before it can grow into a serious resentment:

Suppose that a husband, Alan, likes to keep lots of stuff around, and his wife, Cathy, loathes clutter. He says to her, "I get upset when you dump the oatmeal I was saving. I told you my doctor said it's important for my health to eat oatmeal often." He adds in a respectful tone, "Please leave my oatmeal in the refrigerator." He has just expressed his frustration in a way that honors both his feelings and his wife's. He said what he wants to happen.

Figure 7. Part 4 of a Marriage Meeting: Problems and Challenges

1. Partner A, using I-statements, mentions an area of concern to be discussed.
2. Partner B responds using active listening skills.
3. Once partner A feels understood by B, partner B expresses his or her thoughts and feelings about the subject, while partner A listens actively.

4. Partners continue the discussion until they both feel heard and understood.

| 5a. Agreement is reached. | 5b. Agreement is not yet reached. Partners agree to continue the discussion in the future. | 5c. Partners accept problems that are likely to remain and that they can learn to live with. |

6. If time permits, partners discuss another issue, following steps 1 through 5.

7. Partners conclude the meeting on a positive note, thanking each other for participating.

Note: In early marriage meetings, address only easy-to-resolve problems and challenges. Establish a pattern of successful meetings before trying to resolve a serious relationship issue.

Perhaps Alan's first impulse was to lash out in a "how dare you" tone that would have begun a negative communication. He might have felt tempted to say she was being selfish and inconsiderate, or even to have resorted to name-calling. After all, he has noticed his wife's insensitivity to him about other things.

Instead, Alan allowed himself time to tone down his anger enough to make a constructive I-statement. He began by saying, "I get upset." The word *upset* is often a good choice, because some people become tense when told someone is "angry" or "furious" with them.

Because her husband's words and tone were considerate, Cathy would not have felt a need to defend herself. Her likely response would have been, "I'm sorry. I thought you were done with the oatmeal. From now on I'll leave it alone." She might even have quipped, smiling, "At least until I see mold forming on it, okay?" Cathy might toss in this little joke because occasionally an item in the fridge rots. Alan would smile, too, enjoying her humor, grateful to know that she cares after all and glad to hear that he can expect his oatmeal to stay put. Now he is more likely to notice what's good about his marriage and to tolerate minor annoyances in a spirit of goodwill.

Although Cathy and Alan will continue to have differences about how much clutter is acceptable, their conflict will not be a deal breaker so long as they find ways to address it respectfully.

What Will We Talk About?

During Problems and Challenges, you will want to be able to bring up anything on your mind — once you have established a pattern of successful meetings. You may feel intimidated, not knowing how your partner will respond. Speak up anyway. This is the time to clear the air and seek solutions.

You may want to talk about changing needs, transitions, and intimacy concerns. How will a new work or volunteer schedule affect your relationship? Are you considering having an elderly relative come to live with you? Other developments might be a new job, a move, a child going away to college, or some other change occurring in the household membership.

Does one of you want more together time or crave more alone time? Are you concerned about money? Sex? What new challenges are you anticipating? Keep talking.

Maybe you love the idea of overnight guests, but you've had quite a few lately and feel exhausted. Talk it out. Remember to use I-statements, such as "I want to be hospitable but I'm exhausted from all the overnight company we've had lately." Maybe it's time to say no to potential guests for a while; alternatively, it may work fine to have them if others will agree to pitch in to help with the extra chores. Together, work toward a solution.

You may want to make notes during the week when you notice things that concern you. Write them in a journal or notebook or in another convenient place, secure in the knowledge that you will deal with your issues during your marriage meeting.

Start with Easy-to-Resolve Issues

You may feel tempted to bring up a series of complaints at your initial meeting. This can happen if you have a backlog of concerns that have been building up for some time. Keep in mind, however, that your first goal is for both of you to feel good about holding marriage meetings as a safe way to reconnect each week.

Again, allow time to get used to and feel confident about marriage meetings before bringing up touchy matters. Save those for after you have held several successful meetings. Start with issues that are easy to resolve while keeping the tone light and enjoyable.

Examples of Easy-to-Resolve Concerns

Cathy and Alan's oatmeal situation is one example of a fairly easy-to-resolve concern that is suitable to bring up during an initial or early marriage meeting. Here are a few more that are not likely to raise anyone's hackles, as long as you follow the rules for effective communication described in chapters 7, 8, and 9.

1. Ask if your partner is happy with the meals you've been preparing. Say, "I was wondering whether you'd rather have something different, like more vegetarian dishes or more meat meals?" Or, "How do you feel about meals with less fat and sugar? Would you be willing to try that for a while?"

2. If you're upset by your partner's tendency to be late and you really want to get somewhere on time, you can say, "I would really appreciate it if you can be ready to leave the house with me at 7 PM Saturday night. It means a lot to me to get to the concert on time without feeling rushed."

3. You are struggling to lose weight. Your spouse regularly brings home a large bag of your favorite cookies, placing it right next to the cereal boxes. You can say politely, "Please do me a big favor. The cookies grab me like a magnet, and I'm trying to slim down. I know you really like them, so how about either hiding them somewhere else in the house where I won't see them or, better yet, just keeping them in your office?"

4. If you're ready to hear the answer to this question, you can ask, "Do you feel I'm doing my share of the chores?" Or ask, "What additional chores would you like me to do?" Answers are likely to emerge in the same meeting. If they do not, each of you has the option to say, "I'll need to think about that and tell you next week."

Remember to Save Touchy Topics for Later Meetings

Judy and Wally's story illustrates, again, the risk of introducing an emotionally charged challenge in a marriage meeting before holding a series of successful meetings. During the two years after they got married, Judy had gained about thirty pounds, which had been a source of irritation to Wally, who had watched his formerly slender wife transform into a heavy one. He hadn't told her how disappointed he was, because she kept talking about wanting to lose weight even though it wasn't happening.

Then they held their first marriage meeting. It went fine until they got to Problems and Challenges, when Wally told Judy, "I wish you would stop talking about losing weight and do some things to help yourself. Eat less. Exercise more. It's that simple."

Judy was shocked. Clearly, he had pushed one of her "buttons." She was already self-conscious about her weight. Now she felt hurt and ashamed. With tears in her eyes, she accused Wally of being mean and insensitive.

That was their first and last marriage meeting. Because they had not kept the focus positive, they did not want to schedule another meeting. Judy thought, "Why set myself up to get my feelings hurt?" Wally thought, "I don't want to get criticized for being honest."

In retrospect, what kind of challenge could Wally have introduced initially that would have helped him and his wife look forward to future marriage meetings instead of dreading them? If he had chosen to talk instead about an easier topic, such as asking Judy to support *his* attempt to exercise more, she probably would have been glad to oblige. They might have then talked about getting back to playing tennis together and taking a daily brisk walk. Or he might have asked Judy for ideas about a gift for her upcoming birthday because he wanted to make sure it would be something she would like. She would probably have been glad to help with that challenge!

So save the emotionally charged topics until you have established a pattern of successful meetings with heavy doses of appreciation. Sensitive areas can concern such topics as in-laws, parenting, money, differences in needs for intimacy and time alone, and comments that may come across as critical. Such challenges can take weeks, months, or longer to resolve. Others may linger indefinitely. If an unresolved matter continues to fester, be willing to consult an objective third party, such as a psychotherapist, counselor, clergyperson, or wise, trusted friend.

Discussing a Sensitive Concern

Once you have held enough good, confidence-building meetings, you will be ready to bring up stickier subjects. Here is an example of how a couple discusses a harder challenge effectively, using positive communication skills:

After holding about five marriage meetings, Carol and Roger are getting used to the structure. At first it felt contrived to them, which is typical for many couples. Now they enjoy expressing and receiving appreciation, planning dates, and practicing better teamwork in dealing with chores.

Carol thinks they are ready to talk about a touchy issue. In the past she and Roger have argued about whether she was being too strict or he was being too lenient in disciplining their six-year-old son, Timmy. Carol is now upset because Roger let Timmy come out of his room when he was supposed to still be in a time-out that she had arranged. Carol brings up the subject that evening during the Problems and Challenges part of their marriage meeting.

Calmly, she tells Roger, "I know you enjoy playing catch with Timmy, and he loves it too. Usually I'm happy to see the two of you throwing the ball back and forth. But I was upset today when Timmy was supposed to be in a time-out I had just given him, and then there he was, with you in the backyard...I felt undermined."

Roger defends himself nonchalantly, "Uh, I didn't realize...I thought the time-out was finished."

"Oh, really?" thinks Carol. "Or did you just want to be the good-pal dad again?" But what good would it do to accuse him?

Instead, she simply says, "Please check with me next time before you let him out of his room."

Roger says he will keep that in mind, which Carol understands doesn't mean much. So she says, "I really want you to back me up when I discipline Timmy; I'd like us to act as a team." Roger agrees that next time he will check with her first to find out when the time-out is to end.

Carol realizes that Roger is likely to continue to be a more permissive parent than she. Roger lets Timmy wheedle him into allowing him to stay up well past his bedtime; Carol does not. At the dinner table Carol, not Roger, reminds Timmy to eat his vegetables. She finds it helpful to remember that she was first attracted to Roger because of his kind, easygoing nature. She still loves these traits in him. But now she sees the flip side of these traits: his permissiveness as a parent.

Carol decides it will be helpful to remind Roger in advance when she needs his support in parenting. She realizes that he is likely to continue to be receptive during the Problems and Challenges part of a marriage meeting, which occurs shortly after she has given him sincere compliments during Appreciation.

LIMIT THE NUMBER OF ISSUES YOU BRING UP AND THE MARRIAGE MEETING TO FORTY-FIVE MINUTES

It is usually best to bring up no more than one or two issues during Problems and Challenges. You want to keep the discussion manageable. Avoid the risk of feeling overwhelmed by talking about too many concerns in one sitting. The whole marriage meeting lasts no more than forty-five minutes. Once you become used to holding the meetings, you may find yourselves able to complete them effectively within about thirty minutes or less. Expect to spend no more than about fifteen to twenty minutes on Problems and Challenges. If necessary, use a timer. There is always next week's meeting to continue talking about most topics or to bring up a new one. If necessary, you can schedule a different time to address a concern that requires more discussion to try to resolve.

Questions to Ask Yourself before a Marriage Meeting

Choose carefully what you decide to bring up at your meeting by first asking yourself: Is this a big enough deal to make a fuss about? You might decide to try to accept your spouse's stance or behavior. If you can succeed, great. If not, ask yourself:

1. How crucial is it for me to get my way in this matter? If the two of you are at odds over something, ask yourself to pick a number on a scale of one to ten — *ten* meaning that the matter is very important to you and *one* being unimportant. Then let whoever feels more strongly about the concern have it go his or her way.

2. Are you willing to consider alternative solutions? If yes, brainstorm for more ideas. Then implement a mutually acceptable one. A simple example: about the toilet paper, you might end up agreeing that the best idea is that whoever replaces the roll gets to choose how to set it up. Chapter 9 includes details for how to generate a list of suggestions in order to move toward resolving an issue before deciding which one(s) to implement. Of course, you will want to remember to express appreciation to your spouse for cooperating with you.

Differences Can Help Your Relationship Thrive

Some couples think that a good marriage has no conflict. They say, "We never argue." They think their marriage is in trouble if they don't agree on everything. So they try to cover up their differences with smiles, false expressions of agreement, or silence. Both may unthinkingly say what they suppose their partner wants to hear instead of what they really believe or want. Eventually, they may decide that they've grown apart and that their partner doesn't understand them.

Instead of concealing differences that don't jibe with your fantasy of a perfect marriage, start to notice them. They are a key to a thriving relationship. Whatever irks you now may be the same quality that initially attracted you to your partner. For example, it may drive you crazy when your partner is lax about disciplining the children, the way Carol was bothered about her husband, Roger, in the earlier example. You may feel annoyed when your husband lets the kids stay up way past their bedtime or when he forgets, yet again, to get something you asked him to pick up at the market. But what you liked best about him early on was his gentle, easygoing nature, and you still do.

At times you may feel so blocked or thwarted by a conflict that you think your marriage isn't working. Most likely it is working but there is a need for you to invest more energy in working on it. Identify what specifically is bothering you most. Then ask yourself how you would like it to be different. Paint a picture in your mind of what you want. Next, consider positive ways to address your concern. In time, if not immediately, you can expect to come up with some useful approaches.

Your positive responses to your differences during the Problems and Challenges part of your marriage meeting will restore good feelings and enhance your connection.

Carol and Roger's conversation shows how Carol responded constructively to their different styles of parenting. Roger hadn't backed up Carol when she gave their son a time-out. Roger is the more lenient parent. Carol's nature is more exacting. She values teamwork and discipline. Carol understands that the flip side of

Roger's kind, easygoing personality is his permissiveness with their son. Carol was able to tell Roger respectfully when she felt undermined by him. She was also able to say how she would like him to cooperate with her the next time a similar issue arises. As long as they continue to communicate respectfully and honestly in this area, progress is likely to result, little by little.

WATCH OUT FOR THESE RELATIONSHIP TRAPS

Posted road signs alert drivers to get ready for what's ahead: pedestrians crossing, a curve, or a hairpin turn. Signals also exist that warn us of possible relationship hazards that are easy to miss. Avoid getting caught in these traps, by being alert for them when talking about problems and challenges:

Trap #1: I'm Right; You're Wrong

This attitude signals that one of you is not respecting the other's right to be herself or himself. Many people new to therapy label some of their partner's beliefs, feelings, and behaviors as "wrong," which easily results in a counterattack from the partner. Both spouses in such a situation often want the therapist to serve as referee. I tell them that right and wrong are terms that apply in religious teachings and legal procedures. It is more helpful to view therapy as a time to gain *understanding* of themselves and each other as individuals. Doing so is likely to improve their relationship. Arguments about who is right or wrong breed resentment, which blocks caring and understanding.

When someone who comes to see me for therapy starts out with a right-wrong attitude and finally understands that *different* simply means *not the same*, it feels like a breakthrough. Strive to respect the dignity and essential value of your partner's perspective as well as your own. Only then can you create solutions that satisfy both of you.

By acknowledging differences and responding to relationship challenges constructively during the Problems and Challenges part of your marriage meeting, you will grow as individuals and as a couple.

Trap #2: The Fifty-Fifty Trap

"Shouldn't marriage be a fifty-fifty proposition?" asked a woman in a class I taught.

"Actually no," I said. That kind of thinking causes weighing and measuring. Too much focus on fairness can lead to "what's in it for me" thinking and tit-for-tat nitpicking that sucks the romance and generosity of spirit out of your relationship.

Fairness has its place, but use it sparingly. For example, if you feel resentful about doing the lion's share of the housework, you might ask your partner to help plan a more "fair" way to divide tasks. If you can discuss the subject calmly, do so during the Chores part of your marriage meeting. Otherwise bring it up during Problems and Challenges.

Ideally, both husband and wife focus on doing what pleases the other. Rabbi Manis Friedman shows how to do this, using an example of a couple with a conflict. The husband wants their bedroom window open at night; his wife wants it closed. Here's how they argue: he insists that the window remain closed, and she insists that it be open!

When I heard Rabbi Friedman say this, I was still single and could hardly believe my ears. Until then, I had thought conflicts in marriage consisted of power struggles that lasted until one spouse gave up and let the other "win."

It has been over twenty-five years since I heard Rabbi Friedman's version of how a couple should argue. I still remember what he said because it was so different from my sense of what was possible.

Back then I couldn't imagine letting go of my own strong

preference in order to allow a husband to have it his way. Miraculously, I am able to do this in my marriage — not every time — but much more often than I expected. Fortunately, my husband does this too, and neither of us is counting.

"But isn't marriage all about compromise?" the same woman in my class asked.

Well, not necessarily. When compromise means reaching a middle ground, both parties can lose. Let's say it's date night for a couple. They agree to go out for dinner. The wife wants to go to an Italian restaurant. The husband wants Chinese food. They decide to compromise by going to an American restaurant. Both think that's fair. But each ends up feeling let down to be going out to eat the same old same old. They have achieved a no-win compromise.

Sometimes instead of finding a middle ground it makes more sense for the partner who cares less about something to accommodate the one who cares more. What if you're not sure who cares more? Ask your spouse, "How much do you want that (whatever it is) on a scale of one to ten?" You can ask yourself the same question.

Trap #3: The Martyr Trap

Some people think the key to a good relationship is to be kind and selfless at any cost. What can be wrong with such virtue?

A good relationship is free from too much weighing and measuring. But when the scale tips way out of balance, someone suffers. Being kind and selfless is wonderful as long as doing so does not cause resentment.

A martyr in a marriage typically expects a reward, at least subconsciously. When there is no reciprocation, a martyr feels bitter. It is easy for one spouse to start taking the other's sacrifices for granted, to continue expecting more of the same from the martyr and giving little in return.

Rescue Yourself from the Martyr Trap

Do not wait for someone else to rescue you from the martyr trap. It's a do-it-yourself job. Notice if you are doing more drinking, drug use, or overeating. Other warning signs can be depression, anger, anxiety, decreased interest in sex, insomnia, aches and pains, and lack of energy.

The cure for martyrdom is to become responsible for your own well-being. Learn to balance self-care with concern for your partner. A good marriage supports the growth and vitality of *both* partners. Martyrs drain the life out of themselves and their relationship.

For the sake of your marriage, avoid the martyr trap. If you are feeling overburdened, talk about it during Problems and Challenges after both of you have become comfortable holding marriage meetings. Use positive communication skills. Share your feelings. Say what you would like to be different in your partnership and in your life.

If after trying everything suggested here, you still feel stuck in any of these traps, you may be reenacting a script or pattern you learned in childhood. A skilled therapist can help you recognize and overcome obstacles to healthier functioning and inspire you to create a happier, more fulfilling relationship. An appropriate support group can also be useful for staying on track in how you respond to the joys and challenges of married life.

For more and more couples, the best support of all is the caring, loving relationship that partners create and maintain by holding a weekly marriage meeting.

DOS AND DON'TS FOR PROBLEMS AND CHALLENGES

- *Do* start small. Discuss easy-to-resolve issues during your first few marriage meetings. Once you have become confident about the meetings, you can move on to more sensitive issues.

- *Do* try to limit the number of issues you bring up to no more than one or two at a single meeting.
- *Do* use I-statements. They help prevent the listener from feeling criticized.
- *Do* speak up, even if you are afraid of how your partner may respond.
- *Do* brainstorm for solutions. List and consider many alternatives until one emerges that works for both of you.
- *Do* remember to use the other communication skills explained in detail in chapters 8 and 9: self-talk, congruent communication, nonverbal messages, active listening, constructive criticism and feedback, and brainstorming for solutions.
- *Don't* allow yourself to feel overwhelmed by big, seemingly unsolvable problems. Change takes time, especially for the larger and more sensitive issues. Change takes time and usually happens in baby steps; be patient with the process.
- *Don't* blame. Attack the problem — not each other!

Part III

---◆---

COMMUNICATION SKILLS
for EFFECTIVE MEETINGS

CHAPTER

I-Statements

It is not a lack of love, but a lack of friendship that makes unhappy marriages.

— FRIEDRICH NIETZSCHE

An *I-statement* is a simple, powerful communication skill for expressing your thoughts, feelings, wishes, and needs. I-statements often foster a sense of connection, contentment, and friendship. When you use them while discussing a sensitive issue, you help keep the conversation respectful and can prevent it from turning into an argument.

WHAT IS AN I-STATEMENT?

An I-statement is a clear message that can express what you are thinking, how you are feeling, and why you feel that way. It can be a statement about what you want or need and what you are prepared to do if you don't get it. An I-statement almost always begins with the word *I*.

I-statements are powerful in marriage and elsewhere because they do the following:

- let your spouse know what you want,
- avoid arguments and misunderstandings,
- help you to state your thoughts and feelings calmly, and
- tend to result in increased cooperation (from your spouse, children, and others).

By following the steps of an I-statement listed in the next section, you will be less likely to let your irritation get in the way of gaining your partner's understanding, which is what you really want most, right?

HOW TO MAKE AN I-STATEMENT

Here's a simple formula, paraphrased from one found on the Parenting Wisely website, for making an effective I-statement about a behavior that bothers you:[1]

1. State how you feel about the behavior.
2. Name the specific behavior.
3. Suggest (or say) what you want or don't want to see happen next time.
4. (Optional) Warn of a specific consequence if the behavior continues.

How to Apply the I-Statement Formula
When Talking with Your Spouse

Suppose one of you says to the other, "I feel frustrated when I have to ask you three or four times to take out the kitchen trash. I want you to take it out the first time I mention it. I don't want to nag you."

Now let's break these sentences into the components to include in your I-statements, in accordance with the formula for making them: "I *feel frustrated* (1. state what you are feeling) when I have to ask you three or four times to *take out the kitchen trash* (2. name the specific behavior). *I would like you to notice when the bin is full and take it out promptly or at least take it out the first time I mention it. I don't want to nag you* (3. say what you want or do not want to happen next time).

Regarding number 4, you might want to warn of a specific consequence if your partner continues to forget to empty the garbage, such as "Fruit flies will invade the kitchen if the garbage is allowed to overflow." And you might follow up with a complimentary I-statement, like "I appreciate knowing I can count on you to take care of this."

Although you have the option of using an I-statement to predict a consequence, I recommend that you do so in a way that keeps your goal in mind — which is to gain your partner's cooperation, right? So avoid phrasing your warning in a way that can sound like a threat, such as "I will resent you if you continue to forget to empty the garbage." Instead, keep your focus positive.

Although there is no guarantee that your partner will do what you say you want, your challenge is to ask for it respectfully. If the issue continues to fester regardless, in addition to using I-statements, you can feel confident about using other positive communication skills, described in chapters 8 and 9, to address it.

A You-Statement Is the Opposite of an I-Statement

An I-statement is free from expectations, judgments, and blame. It is a clear expression of how the situation looks from your side (your feelings, beliefs, thoughts, wants, needs) and how you would like it to be.

In contrast, a you-statement sounds judgmental or demanding. You-statements put the recipient on the defensive. Examples: "You always..., you never..., you should..., you shouldn't..., you're wrong..."

How to Begin an I-Statement

Here are some specific ways to begin an I-statement:

- I appreciate...
- I like...
- I want...
- I'd rather not...
- I feel...(happy, hurt, anxious, resentful, grateful, sad, uncomfortable, loving, confused, overwhelmed — or state a different emotion) when you...(action word) because... (note the effect the action or event had on you).
- What I would like instead is...

Do You React or Respond?

Think about how you and your partner communicate about sensitive topics. If your partner asks or possibly insists that you do something you don't want to do, what happens? Do you ignore the tightness you feel inside, either in your chest or elsewhere? Do you change the subject? Do you accuse your spouse of being selfish, unreasonable, inconsiderate, or stupid? Or do you put up a wall of indifference? If you behave in any of these ways, you are *reacting* rather than responding and you might be straining your relationship.

Reacting means doing or saying the first thing that pops into your mind. If you routinely, without protesting, react to your partner by doing whatever you are asked or told to do, even when you don't want to, you are likely to build up resentment. If, instead, you react by belittling or stonewalling your mate, he or she will probably feel intimidated, offended, and anxious.

By responding thoughtfully instead of reacting impulsively, you can create a receptive, friendly climate in which good feelings flourish all around.

Example: Eva Keeps Her Reaction to Herself, Then Responds

Eva's husband, Spencer, says he'd like for them to see the latest R-rated thriller movie. Her throat tightens as she thinks, "He's so insensitive. He knows I can't fall asleep after seeing blood and guts on a big screen; I've told him before." She immediately judges her husband as callous and clueless. Having such thoughts now and then is normal, but what should she do with them? She might be tempted to react by blurting out, "You're selfish. You know I hate violent movies and that they keep me awake at night. You only care about yourself." But what good would that do?

Eva decides to take the high road. She knows that criticizing Spencer might relieve her irritation at the moment but would decrease trust and create distance between them. So she accepts her immediate feelings and thoughts, then takes a few breaths and closes her eyes to center herself. She thinks about how to *respond* respectfully, to both herself and her husband. She does this by making I-statements. She gently tells Spencer, "I cringe at the thought of going to a horror movie. I'd like you either to suggest movies we can both expect to enjoy or to ask me what I would like to see." Eva also can suggest a different movie or other activity she thinks both of them would enjoy.

STRIVE FOR PROGRESS, NOT PERFECTION

Assuming that you are a nice person but not a saint, you can expect to slip into a reactive mode at times and say or do something you regret. When this happens, recognize your mistake and do the repair work promptly. Be generous with your I-statements. Let your partner know that you regret your behavior by saying sincerely in a way that fits for you, "I am sorry. I wish I could erase what I said. I will try to do better next time."

Beware of Disguised You-Statements

"I feel that you are wrong" and "I think you should" are *disguised you-statements*. "I disagree with you," "I have a different opinion," "I would like you to...," and "I prefer..." are true I-statements.

If tempted to make a you-statement, change it into an I-statement.

Example of How to Change a You-Statement into an I-Statement

Amy's mother-in-law routinely criticizes her during visits. Amy's husband, Ned, is present at these times but says nothing. Amy feels awful about this but doesn't confront her mother-in-law, because she wants her to like her. Meanwhile, her stomach churns and her breathing becomes shallow.

Amy is also upset with Ned for not supporting her. She thinks he may secretly agree with his mother's put-downs of her for being "overweight," for being a "sloppy housekeeper," and for acting like a "spoiled brat" who sets a bad example for their toddler by insisting on getting her way.

Alone with Ned later, Amy has an urge to say, "You never defend me when your mother criticizes me. You're a wimp. You act like a helpless little boy around her." Lashing out like this would be cathartic — it would bring a quick feeling of relief.

But how would Ned respond to such you-statements? He might attack her in kind with some of his own, saying, "You're too sensitive," or "You actually could stand to lose a few pounds." Or he could silently stew, resenting Amy for implying he's not a good enough husband and for calling him a name. He might think, "I'll show her," and then figure out a way to get even.

Aware of these risks, Amy does a mental 180-degree turn. She decides to use I-statements. She takes a few deep breaths and chooses her words. She tells Ned calmly, "I feel hurt and abandoned by you when you don't defend me when your mother criticizes me. When she gets on my case, I want you to support me."

Amy has said how she feels and what she wants. She has cleared the air. She hopes that next time his mother mentions her weight, Ned will say, "I love every ounce of her just the way she is." Regardless of whether Ned defends her in the future, Amy has communicated in a positive way how she feels and what she wants. Chapter 11 describes how Amy resolves her mother-in-law issue.

WHEN I-STATEMENTS BACKFIRE

In most instances, you can expect to be pleased with how your partner responds to your I-statements. You have opened up and allowed yourself to be vulnerable, a prerequisite for intimacy. Your connection gets strengthened when you feel heard, valued for your true self, and understood.

However, in some situations, I-statements backfire. Some people feel uncomfortable with them. They may have been told by their parents that it is selfish to ask directly for what you want. They might have been criticized as children for expressing angry, hurt, or sad feelings and been told it is "wrong" to feel that way. In that case, they learned that it is not safe to allow themselves to be vulnerable, which is what we are doing when we express our true feelings.

Instead of staying tuned in to their deepest, truest selves, they learned to use less healthy ways of trying to cope, such as withdrawing, rebelling, or bullying. Such a person can easily grow into an adult who, lacking self-understanding, will find it difficult to empathize with an intimate partner.

If this scenario describes your spouse, he or she may feel backed into a corner upon hearing your I-statements and then respond insensitively.

To illustrate this idea, suppose that Amy's husband, Ned, was punished as a child for expressing his feelings and for asking directly for what he wanted. When Amy said she felt hurt by his silence and that she wanted his support, he might have come back with "You shouldn't feel that way. You're too sensitive. You should just get used to her." Or he may have said, "She's right. You have gotten fat. You are not a good housekeeper. You are a bad example for Jimmy."

PRACTICE HELPS OVERCOME OBSTACLES TO MAKING I-STATEMENTS

In case you and your partner are not yet able to communicate effectively with I-statements, practice is likely to help. By continuing to use them and respond positively on hearing them, you can expect to become more comfortable with them. If serious challenges are holding you back from empathizing with yourself and your partner, recognize that entrenched patterns are usually not possible to change on your own. If you want to create a healthier relationship, seek individual or couple therapy to help achieve your goal.

I-STATEMENTS ARE YOUR FOUNDATION

With practice, you can master the art of making I-statements. Be patient with yourself and your partner as you gain comfort in communicating this way. Once you gain this skill, you will have a solid foundation for using the communication skills described in the next two chapters. Each technique will serve you well during marriage meetings and at other times.

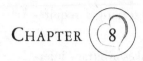

CHAPTER 8

Self-Talk

People don't just get upset. They contribute to their upsetness.

— ALBERT ELLIS

For a good marriage, who is the most important person with whom you should be communicating well? If you think it's your spouse, think again. The most important person to converse with constructively is *yourself*!

You need not try to resolve every situation by talking it over with your partner. Self-talk refers to the messages we say to ourselves. You can change destructive messages you tell yourself into supportive ones. Here is the five-step method proposed by psychologist Pamela Butler, PhD, author of *Talking to Yourself: How Cognitive Behavior Therapy Can Change Your Life*:

Step 1. *Be aware.* Listen to your own self-talk.

Step 2. *Evaluate.* Decide if your inner dialogue is supportive or destructive.

Step 3. *Identify.* Determine the source of the cognitive distortion or thinking error that is maintaining your inner speech. Is it

- the Driver, an inner self who commands you to be perfect, hurry up, be strong, please others, or try hard;

- the Stopper, an inner self who catastrophizes, self-labels, self-judges in negative ways, and sets rigid requirements; or
- the Confuser, an inner self who makes arbitrary inferences, fails to be aware of the full picture, overgeneralizes, and makes other cognitive distortions?

Step 4. *Support yourself.* Replace your negative self-talk with permission and self-affirmation. For example, if you are inclined to please others too often at your own expense, you can replace negative self-talk with permission by saying, "At times it is important for me to do or say what I want, even if my doing so does not please my partner at the moment."

Step 5. *Develop your guide.* Decide what action you need to take, based on your new supportive position.

WIFE'S SELF-TALK BRINGS APPRECIATION FOR HER HUSBAND

In this example, a wife uses self-talk when she is in a funk over the fact that her husband stays in a relatively low-paying job when she believes he could earn much more elsewhere. She asks herself these five questions, as suggested by Dr. Butler, and answers each one:

1. *What am I telling myself?* "I'm telling myself that my husband isn't good enough; he's lazy. With his ability and experience, he should have a job that pays more. But he just stays where he is earning a lot less than he could."

2. *Is my self-talk helping?* "No, it is not, because it's making me resent my husband."

3. *Is the Driver, Stopper, or Confuser operating?* "My Confuser is causing me to fail to be aware of the full picture."

4. *What permission and self-affirmation will I give myself?* "I

give myself permission to be aware of the full picture: My husband purposely chose a low-stress job because he wants to be able to relax evenings and weekends. I like his easygoing nature and was attracted to him in the first place because of it. I wouldn't be happy married to a competitive type who comes home from work all stressed out."

5. *What action will I take based on my new supportive position?* "I will remember to appreciate having a husband who comes home in a good mood, talks to me, spends time with our children, and does chores. If I am concerned about money, I will economize or figure out a way to earn more myself."

This example shows the effectiveness of communicating with yourself. It was more constructive for this wife to recognize and transform her self-talk into a more supportive message than to confront her husband about what had been bothering her.

By applying the five steps of self-talk, we can catch ourselves making negative assumptions about our self or our spouse that may not be correct. If we skip the five-step process, it is easy to jump from an unhelpful thought to resentment, self-pity, or other destructive behaviors that are based on a false interpretation of our partner's behavior.

HUSBAND'S SELF-TALK HELPS OVERCOME PANIC ABOUT HIS MARRIAGE

In this example, a husband feels upset because his wife has not been responding recently to his attempts to converse with her. She looks annoyed and answers his questions in monosyllables. The husband's initial thought is "She doesn't love me anymore." He feels distraught and fears she'll leave him. It crosses his mind to consult an attorney to clarify his legal rights.

Realizing he is working himself up to a panic, he decides to use self-talk. First he recognizes that thinking his wife no longer loves him is *not helpful,* because it is making him feel insecure about his marriage. He determines that his Stopper is operating, causing him to *catastrophize* — that is, to assume the worst. He then gives himself permission to come up with this more realistic, helpful message to himself: "I remember that she told me last night that her job has become really stressful lately because she is covering for a vacationing coworker. She is on the phone all day and barely gets any downtime. I can see how she wouldn't feel like chatting after a day like that. We still love each other." He decides on an action plan: he will give her as much space as she needs. He decides also to offer to give her a back massage, a cup of tea, or something else she might like.

Can you see how the self-talk technique can prevent you from wallowing in destructive thoughts, which easily lead to hurt feelings; reactive, "I'll show you" behaviors; and other actions that distance you from your partner?

The importance of self-talk cannot be overstated. By using this skill at the right times, you are likely to become more receptive and empathic toward yourself and your spouse.

CHAPTER  9

More Communication Techniques for Marriage Meetings

The single biggest problem with communication is the illusion that it has taken place.

— GEORGE BERNARD SHAW

Every part of a marriage meeting, and particularly Problems and Challenges, will go more smoothly when you use these communication skills, along with I-statements:

- Congruent communication
- Nonverbal messages
- Active listening
- Constructive criticism and feedback
- Brainstorming for solutions

As you get used to communicating using these skills during marriage meetings, you can expect to apply them in normal, everyday conversations with your spouse and others. Let's take a look at how to apply each technique.

CONGRUENT COMMUNICATION

Congruent communication is the healthiest kind for a close relationship with a partner and with other important people in your life. It occurs when the speaker's message is authentic and mutually respectful. It fosters a feeling of closeness or connection. Communication that is not congruent creates distance.

At times, most of us slip into incongruent ways of relating, especially when feeling stressed. Notice when you are doing this, because you can then put energy into restoring the connection with congruent messages. Virginia Satir, a founder of the family therapy movement, has specified five ways people communicate when disagreement exists, and emphasizes the value of congruent communication. The five ways are listed here with paraphrased explanations:[1]

Five Types of Communication People Use
When Disagreement Exists

1. **Congruent**

   When our communication is congruent, we are expressing ourselves clearly and directly. We convey respect both for ourselves and for the other person. I-statements are congruent when the speaker's tone and body language match the spoken words. I-statements express the speaker's feelings, wishes, likes, and dislikes. People who communicate congruently accept that their relationship partner can have feelings and preferences that differ from their own. Examples of congruent statements: "I feel...," "I want...," "I would like..." The speaker is being assertive, not aggressive or passive.

2. **Blaming**

   This type of communication is an attempt to dominate the other person. You-statements of a critical nature are common in it. Examples: "You should (or shouldn't)...,"

"You always (or never)..." The speaker is basically saying, "You're wrong." Name-calling is a form of blaming.

3. **Placating**

   Placating is an attempt to avoid conflict with someone by holding back from expressing ourselves honestly. It happens when we "go along in order to get along." But when we hold back from expressing to a partner our important true feelings, beliefs, and needs, we are likely to feel frustrated and resentful as a result. Examples: "Whatever you say...," "Okay," and other expressions of agreement *when you do not really agree.*

4. **Reasonable**

   Someone who is being "reasonable" (in this context) focuses on logic and ignores feelings. Such people want things to make sense. However, feelings are facts. They do not need to appear logical. You may have heard the expression "There is no accounting for personal taste." Examples of "reasonable" statements: "You shouldn't feel that way because...," "You should have gotten over that by now," "How could you like (or want) *that?*"

5. **Irrelevant**

   The person whose communication is irrelevant deflects the conversation instead of responding sensitively. Uncomfortable hearing what a partner has said, he or she may make a joke or change the subject.

For a warm, loving relationship, strive for congruent communication. Be gentle with yourself when you find that you have related less positively. It is normal to do this now and then. Notice when it happens. Then you can make a correction that will help the two of you to reconnect, such as by offering a sincere apology.

After I explained the concept of congruent communication to Zack, he said, "We didn't have much of that in my family." He and his partner, Wendy, were able to complete a marriage meeting in my office only one time out of several attempts. He sometimes provoked her to cry by calling her "lazy" and "a slob."

Zack wanted to learn to communicate his feelings congruently. His therapy sessions gradually helped him recognize and accept whatever feelings came up for him. In time he began to practice using positive communication techniques, especially I-statements, to express himself. More details about how he and Wendy improved their relationship appear in chapter 13.

We learn to communicate from our earliest teachers, our parents, who were taught by theirs, and so on. If you wish they had shown you better ways to relate, also give them credit for having done the best they were able to do with the knowledge they had at the time.

Now it's up to you. Changing a habitual way of behaving takes time, determination, practice, and sometimes professional help. You can succeed!

Nonverbal Messages

Many of us think that the words we say determine the bulk of the message people receive from us. However, studies by Albert Mehrabian, PhD, and colleagues confirm the truth of the familiar saying "It's not what you say; it's how you say it."[2]

Here is what the study found regarding how much of the message received by the listener is based on the sender's words, voice, and body language when people are communicating about their feelings and attitudes:

Spoken words: 7 percent

Voice tone: 38 percent

Body language: 55 percent

Voice tone includes volume and inflection. Examples of body language include eye contact or the lack of it, facial expressions, body position (such as facing toward or turned away from the other person, arms open or crossed), and posture.

So during your marriage meeting, be aware of your voice, facial expressions, and body language, as well as of the words you say. Remember to smile when you express appreciation and to look your partner in the eye when you want to connect. Use a friendly, soft voice if you want to come across as accepting and compassionate, even when discussing a problem or challenge. When you sit side by side, rather than across from each other, you help foster a sense of cooperation.

ACTIVE LISTENING

Active listening involves more than just lending an ear to your partner.[3] It requires complete concentration, giving space to the other person, and not injecting your own thoughts and feelings into the moment. It can take some self-control to hear what your partner wants to say and to postpone stating your own thoughts for a moment. While the technique may strike you as rather formal for a loving relationship, using it as directed is likely to foster emotional closeness and more acceptance and understanding of each other's point of view.

How to Listen Actively

First, make sure that the conversation about a potentially sensitive topic occurs when both of you are calm and distractions are unlikely to occur. Then follow these six steps:

1. Stop what you are doing. Take the necessary time out to really listen to your partner.
2. Look at your partner. Making eye contact tells your partner that you are ready to listen. Body language and facial expression also indicate an interest in listening. Make sure

that the nonverbal signals you send reflect a willingness to listen. Focus on your partner. Try to push everything else from your mind.

3. Listen to your partner. Listen without interrupting, arguing, or giving advice. Just listen. Notice if you are having a strong emotional reaction to your partner's words. If yes, breathe in and out slowly a few times to center yourself. You will have a chance to express yourself later, but for now just listen.

4. Rephrase or repeat what your partner says. This step encourages us to be good listeners. It also helps us to understand the other person's meaning and feelings. Rephrasing also helps the partner to recognize and clarify her or his feelings. Start with "I hear you saying..." Always check out with your partner whether your interpretation of what was communicated is accurate. Ask, "Am I correctly understanding what you are saying?" The speaker should clarify his or her meaning if the partner's interpretation seems inaccurate, after which step 4 should be repeated.

5. Be empathic. Seek to understand your spouse's emotions in the situation she or he is describing. Try to put yourself in your spouse's position. Save your advice for another time. Some people are afraid that if they are empathic they will have to give in to or agree with their partner. It is important to recognize that what we all want most is to feel *understood*.

Reversing Speaker-Listener Roles

After completing the above exercise to the point that your spouse clearly feels understood by you, you may want to express your viewpoint on the topic. If so, reverse roles. Share your own thoughts and feelings while your partner practices active listening.

CONSTRUCTIVE CRITICISM AND FEEDBACK

Constructive criticism occurs in a context of support and appreciation. It helps us to improve ourselves and grow. Its opposite, destructive criticism, feels like faultfinding and finger-pointing and typically results in a defensive response.

In each situation, notice the positive features. We all want to be appreciated for what we are doing well. Here is how to sugarcoat the pill that might otherwise taste bitter:

1. Before offering your comments, observations, or suggestions, ask your partner whether she or he is willing to receive them. If your spouse shows no interest in accepting your offer, do not continue the discussion. If your partner says yes, go to step 2.

2. When you give constructive feedback, use the "sandwich" approach — along with I-statements — by arranging your comments in the following order:

    a. First, say something positive. State at least one thing you appreciate about your partner. For example, "I like the way you give me a warm hug when you arrive home from work."

    b. Next, state your concern about what your partner did or didn't do that caused you to feel upset or uncomfortable. Using the example given here, you might say, "I don't like it when you read the mail before you give me a hello hug."

    c. Describe what you would like to have happen instead, such as by saying, "I would like us to hug when you get home before you get involved in anything else."

    d. Finally, say something else that is complimentary about your partner. You might say, "Hugging you is one of the highlights of my day."

3. If you are the receiver of the criticism, follow the instructions for active listening.

BRAINSTORMING FOR SOLUTIONS

Do you sometimes feel like you and your spouse are locking horns? This tends to happen when each of you has a different fixed idea about how things should go, about money, parenting, sex, recreation, or something else.

Brainstorming for solutions tends to unlock the horns. The process can resolve lingering disagreements and foster win-win solutions that take into consideration the viewpoints of both partners.

If you're like me, you're doing some brainstorming already, even if it is not structured as described here. Let's say I'm faced with a challenging situation. I might instinctively act on the first idea that comes to mind. But if I want to be more thorough, I wrack my brain for several possible ways to respond. I might also ask other people what they think, gathering enough suggestions until the "right" one emerges.

A friend once wryly observed that I ask everyone for their opinions and then do what I want. From her point of view, my asking others was a waste of time. But I viewed it differently. In my own way, I was brainstorming. Sometimes the solution came from my own mind; other times from someone else's.

Corporations often use a more structured brainstorming process in order to make good decisions for their companies. This method also works beautifully for couples seeking to resolve differences in a way that satisfies both of them and therefore benefits their relationship.

First Listen Actively

To create an optimal climate for brainstorming, strive to respect differences in a positive spirit. Make sure that you understand each other's take on the issue that you find challenging. Sometimes it is hard to do this. We may be so full of our own opinion that we have no room to take in our partner's reasoning. By carefully using the active listening technique described earlier, you can take in your partner's way of thinking.

So before the two of you start to brainstorm, do listen to what each other says. Recognize where there is disagreement and accept it. Avoid the common mistake of casting blame or telling your partner that he or she is wrong.

Example: How to Define the Problem in a Way
That Regards Each Opinion as Valid

Diane and Tyler differed about whether to involve their children in planning their next family vacation. Tyler insisted that they, the parents, should decide on their own where the family would go. Diane maintained that the right thing to do would be to involve the children.

Tyler initially defined the problem by saying that his wife was too lenient a parent. Diane defined it by saying her husband was too strict. Each was saying in effect that the other's way of thinking was wrong. Tyler and Diane felt blamed and judged negatively by each other. At this point, how could they have been expected to cooperate enough to brainstorm effectively? Both probably would have shut down and reached a stalemate.

Let's suppose that Tyler and Diane remember that active listening can help people get past a deadlock. Tyler tells Diane that in his family, his parents always made the decisions about vacations without asking the children what they wanted. He never expected to have a say back then. He's afraid they will be "spoiling" the children if they start asking them what they think, making them become self-centered monsters.

Diane tells him that she hears him saying that he grew up

without having input into such decisions, and that he thinks giving their children a say about the vacation will spoil them. Then she checks in with Tyler to make sure she got it right. Tyler says yes.

Now it's Tyler's turn to listen. Diane says that in her family she and her brother were asked for their opinions, and their parents took them into consideration when planning a family vacation. She liked feeling that her parents cared about what she wanted and felt closer to them because of that.

Tyler then tells Diane accurately what he just heard her say.

Once both partners feel understood, they can label the challenge more objectively. In this case, it became "How will we plan a vacation that takes into consideration one partner's desire for only the parents to choose where they go and the other partner's desire to involve their children in the decision?"

After considering various options during brainstorming, they resolved the issue with this solution: "We will ask our children for their vacation preferences, making it clear to them that we, their parents, will make the final decision."

How to Brainstorm for Solutions in a Marriage Meeting

Here's how the brainstorming process works, step-by-step:

1. Define and write down the issue in a way that respects the validity of both partners' viewpoints.
2. Solicit suggestions and fresh thinking, and *do not make judgments*.
3. List each idea on a piece of paper, on a whiteboard, or in whatever visible way works for you.
4. While remaining receptive to new ideas, partners look over the completed list.
5. Together, partners decide whether the first suggestion is worth considering.

6. If either partner vetoes it, eliminate it by drawing a line through it.
7. Repeat the process, going down the list.
8. After finishing steps 5 through 7, partners assess pros and cons of each idea still on the list.
9. Partners rank the remaining possible solutions.
10. Partners circle the idea(s) they decide to implement.

EXAMPLE OF A COUPLE BRAINSTORMING FOR A SOLUTION

Carlos was upset with his wife for keeping their garage so full of her "junk" that there was no room for his car. Maria treasured her scrapbooks, photo albums, spare cookware, boxes of hobby supplies, and other paraphernalia. Seeing how upset she got when he complained, he continued to put up with the situation, but unhappily.

At a Marriage Meeting workshop, Carlos and Maria volunteered to be guided by me through the brainstorming process while the other couples watched.

First I asked them to use the active listening communication technique and tell each other how they felt about the garage situation and how they would like it to be.

Almost in tears, Maria said, "I feel nervous when you say you want me to get rid of things. My scrapbooks and photo albums are treasures. I need the sewing machine, art supplies, my bike, clothes for when I lose weight, and extra sets of dishes. Our kids will be glad to pass on their saved toys and outgrown outfits to their future children. I want to keep almost everything."

Touched by her emotion, Carlos replied, "I hear you saying that what you have in the garage is really important to you and also might benefit our future grandchildren."

Once Maria and Carlos had conversed respectfully, and long

enough for both of them to feel understood, they were ready to begin the brainstorming process. Here is how it went, step-by-step:

1. First, I suggested that they define their challenge in a way that accepted both viewpoints as valid. They agreed to this wording: "How can we live together in harmony when one of us likes to fill the garage with her things and the other likes it to be empty enough for his car to be inside?"

2. Then, we listed suggestions for solutions. I encouraged fresh thinking, asking the couple and other workshop participants to toss in their ideas. If anyone said, "No" or "That won't work," I reminded them that we needed to accept all suggestions for the time being while keeping an open mind, no matter how disagreeable or off the wall they might seem. Here is the list that resulted:
   - Rent a storage space.
   - Divide the garage in half.
   - All that fits in the attic goes there. The rest gets tossed.
   - Move to a place with a much bigger garage.
   - Have a yard sale.
   - Put a storage hut in the yard.
   - Jointly pare down.
   - Do nothing.
   - Wait for rats.
   - Organize. Get boxes and install a storage system with shelves.
   - Bring in a professional organizer.

3. As each suggestion was offered, I wrote it on a whiteboard.

4. I instructed Carlos and Maria to stay open-minded as they looked over the completed list.

5. Next, I asked them to look at the first suggestion (rent a storage space) and decide whether it might be a possible solution.

6. I told them that if either of them vetoed it, it would get crossed off. Neither wanted to pay to rent a storage space, so I drew a line through it.

7. We repeated the process, going down the list, crossing out whatever either spouse vetoed.

8. Next, Carlos and Maria evaluated the suggestions that remained on the list, noting pros and cons.

9. Then from these suggestions, they chose the ones they were ready to act upon. Finally, they chose the two suggestions they felt ready to implement.

Here is what their list looked like after they crossed out the solutions vetoed by one or both of them:

- ~~Rent a storage space.~~
- ~~Divide the garage in half.~~
- ~~All that fits in the attic goes there. The rest gets tossed.~~
- ~~Move to a place with a much bigger garage.~~
- ~~Have a yard sale.~~
- ~~Put a storage hut in the yard.~~
- Jointly pare down.
- ~~Do nothing.~~
- ~~Wait for rats.~~
- Get boxes and install a storage system with shelves. Organize.
- Bring in a professional organizer.

They both liked the "jointly pare down" suggestion, which involved going through everything in the garage and seeing what each of them was willing to eliminate. They also liked the idea of getting boxes and shelves to organize what would remain in the garage. They agreed to bring in a professional organizer only if they were not able to succeed on their own. They ranked their preferences for a solution in this order:

A. Jointly pare down.
B. Get boxes and shelves to organize.
C. Hire a professional organizer if necessary.

The Brainstorming-for-a-Solution Technique Can Be Used for Concerns Introduced Earlier

The brainstorming technique typically fits into the Problems and Challenges part of a marriage meeting. It can be helpful to use this method to address emotionally charged or complex concerns that were mentioned earlier in the meeting and got moved to Problems and Challenges.

For example, suppose a challenging issue arises during the Chores part of the meeting. One partner may say she or he thinks the chores are not being divided fairly. During Plan for Good Times, differences may arise about where to go on a vacation. During Appreciation, one partner may be upset with the other and withhold appreciation.

In each case, simply move the emotionally charged topic to Problems and Challenges. Then use the active listening skill. Doing this might be enough to resolve the issue. If not, you may well create a solution by brainstorming and have fun in the process.

Part IV

—·◆·—

Transforming Relationships
with Marriage Meetings

CHAPTER  10

Opposites Attract, and Then What?

KEN AND LAUREN

Often the qualities that initially attract us to our partner have a flip side that eventually irritates us. A husband feels valued at first because of his wife's requests for his help in making decisions about small things. But after a while, he resents her for being needy and insecure. A woman is thrilled by how her boyfriend flirts with her in the beginning. But after marriage, she has fits of jealousy when he teasingly chats up other women.

The story in this chapter shows how a couple used the marriage meeting tool and techniques to manage conflicts that reflected their different temperaments, which had felt complementary in the beginning but later became a source of irritation.

● ◆ ●

Before they got married, Lauren adored Ken's easygoing nature and wry sense of humor. Ken loved Lauren's enthusiasm. She was a spark that lit him up, whether she was suggesting fun for the two of them or talking about a new development at work. They felt right together, talking and laughing.

A corporate attorney, Lauren drove herself hard. Ken was the perfect antidote to the stress she built up. She supposed he was a calming presence at the college where he taught philosophy.

Lauren's first hint of trouble came when she and Ken were planning their wedding. Actually, she felt as if *she* were planning the wedding. Sometimes she wanted to scream. When they met with the caterer to decide on the menu for the reception, Lauren was full of questions: "Should the meal be buffet style or served to guests at their tables?" "Should the appetizers include meat as well as fish?" "What will we do for vegetarians?" Ken looked like he'd rather be elsewhere. When Lauren asked what he thought about this detail or that, he shrugged, yawned, or looked into space.

Choices had to be made. "What kind of partnership is this?" Lauren thought. "I have to think of everything by myself."

CONFLICTS ABOUT CHORES

Lauren values predictability and attention to details. She expects agreements to be kept. During their courtship she saw Ken as carefree. After marriage she began to see him as *careless.*

One day Ken said he would change a lightbulb after dinner. The next evening, Lauren curled up in a chair by the lamp, eager to read a novel. She clicked the lamp's switch. Nothing. "I can't trust him to keep a simple agreement," she thought. "He's lazy and selfish."

At first Lauren had been understanding. She knew anyone could make a mistake. But Ken was forgetting too often. If she asked him to pick up four ripe avocadoes on his way home so she could make guacamole for company that night, he might bring home two rock-hard ones with no explanation or forget the avocadoes altogether. Ken didn't keep to-do lists, an appointment book, or any other time-management system.

After Lauren told Ken, for the fourth or fifth time, "You're being passive-aggressive," he burst out, "I resent that. You're being unfair." Slamming his book on the table, he stormed out of the room.

Feeling uncared for, Lauren became less interested in sex. Ken felt frustrated, but he wasn't the type to complain. Distance grew between them. Had Ken and Lauren reached an impasse?

Not an impasse. They were at a *crossroads*. Depending on how they addressed their conflicts, their relationship could improve or deteriorate. Both Ken and Lauren longed for the caring relationship they had enjoyed while dating and during their honeymoon. They learned about marriage meetings and decided to try them out.

Marriage Meetings Make a Difference

Before they started holding the weekly meetings, Ken felt like he could never please Lauren. She criticized him for what he thought were honest mistakes like forgetting. She nagged him about trivia like changing a lightbulb or gathering papers needed for tax preparation. "What's the big rush? I said I'd get to it," he would think. "Why can't she trust me?"

Ken and Lauren say that their marriage meetings have helped them restore trust and intimacy. "I'm the kind of person who needs closure," Lauren explains. "My mind feels cluttered when it's full of things left hanging. Because Ken tolerates loose ends better than me, I'm willing to be the one who initiates most of our meetings. If he says he wants to start ten minutes later than our agreed-on time, I say okay."

Lauren and Ken Conduct Part 1 of the Marriage Meeting: Appreciation

Ken, the less verbal partner, expresses appreciation first, telling Lauren, for example, "I liked it when you smiled at me from across the room at the party on Sunday. I felt treasured by you. I appreciate you for making the delicious burritos for dinner last night. I appreciate your consideration in phoning me Monday to say you'd be home late. I appreciate you for buying the new blue dress last Tuesday that you look so hot in. I like how the blue matches your eyes."

On hearing Ken's last compliment, Lauren sighs with relief and smiles. She had felt guilty about spending so much on the dress. Now she thinks, "He's glad I bought it!" When Ken asks whether he left anything out, she says no and thanks him.

Here are a few examples of Lauren's compliments to Ken: "I appreciate your patience in listening to me talk about my pressures at work yesterday. I appreciate your kindness in giving me that fantastic foot massage Wednesday, right after I got home and was so tired. I appreciate you for remembering to stop at the store on your way home and bring the lettuce I asked for. I appreciate you for encouraging me to see the play with you Saturday night. I liked it a lot. I like how handsome you look with your new haircut; it shows off your chiseled features."

Ken sits up straighter on hearing Lauren's last compliment. She then thinks he looks even more appealing. Both now feel relaxed and valued.

At first it felt a bit awkward to them to talk this way, but it became easier with practice. Also, a nice ripple effect occurred in everyday life. As Lauren became used to complimenting Ken during their marriage meetings, she became more aware at other times of his positive traits and behaviors. Now she tells him often when she likes what he does. She compliments his appearance when he dresses well. She thanks him for favors he does for her and makes sure to express appreciation each time he gets what she asked for from the market.

Ken has started bringing Lauren flowers. Even if they are not the kind she has told him she likes best, she thanks him sweetly. At first she felt like she was acting, but over time it became natural. As she learned in the Marriage Meeting workshop: appreciate your partner's *effort* to please you, even if he doesn't do it perfectly.

Teamwork Challenge

Ken didn't stop being forgetful overnight. During the Chores part of one of their first marriage meetings, he said he would phone their accountant during the week to schedule a tax preparation appointment. When Lauren asked him about that at their next meeting, he said he forgot to make the call. A week later, again he said he had forgotten.

Lauren kept her appointment book handy during their marriage meetings. She suggested that Ken get one and note when he would do whatever task was on his to-do list. Ken resisted, saying, "I'll remember this time. Don't worry."

"How can a smart thirty-seven-year-old man not have an appointment book?" Lauren thought, but said nothing. Criticizing him then would have derailed the meeting.

She and Ken had been careful to put off discussing controversial topics until after establishing a series of successful meetings. Now, in their sixth meeting, they followed the instruction to discuss sensitive concerns like this one during Problems and Challenges.

Respecting Both Partners' Personalities and Interests When Planning Dates

During the third part of the marriage meeting, Plan for Good Times, Lauren and Ken routinely plan weekly dates. Lauren likes looking forward to them; Ken is more of a spur-of-the-moment type. They have learned to accommodate each other. Sometimes they make a specific plan for a date, such as arranging to see a certain play on a Saturday night. Other times they leave it open-ended by agreeing during their marriage meeting when their next date will occur, but waiting until it is closer to that time to plan what they will do on it. They also mention enjoyable activities they plan to do individually, such as a golf outing for Ken and a water exercise class for Lauren.

Lauren Uses the "Sandwich Approach"
to Improve Teamwork

Ken's absent-minded-professor style annoyed Lauren to no end. Yet she knew from experience that calling him lazy, forgetful, or passive-aggressive would hurt their relationship. At some point she asked herself, "How can I help him to keep his agreements?"

Ken had already told Lauren during the Chores part of their marriage meeting that he had never used an appointment book and saw no need for one. When they resumed talking about this during Problems and Challenges, Lauren used the sandwich approach, beginning with a compliment. She said, "Ken, you know I love your easygoing nature. I feel so comfortable with you almost always."

Next, she said what she did not want: "I don't want to feel like I'm asking you to do something you don't want to do." Then she said what she wanted and how she felt when she didn't get it: "But I want to be able to trust you. When you don't do what you say, like with the tax preparer, I feel frustrated."

Ken told her, "You're being unfair. Anyone can make a mistake."

Lauren agreed that we all make mistakes, then added gently, "I would really like for you to use an appointment book or some other system to keep track of things you say you'll do."

Lauren finished the sandwich with a compliment and by expressing optimism: "I know you are responsible about the most important things. I like it that you always pay the bills on time, for example. I think we'll both be happier once you have a time-management system in place so the little things will get handled more smoothly. I would be lost myself without my appointment book."

Ken looked receptive but not quite convinced. Lauren offered to buy him whatever system he would be willing to try using. He said he'd rather get it himself. He did and brought it to their next marriage meeting. Lauren smiled, told him this meant a lot to her, and thanked him.

Ken and Lauren's example illustrates how, by using the marriage meeting's structure and some of its prescribed communication skills, they succeeded in gaining closure on a long-standing issue. First, they established a series of successful meetings during which they avoided talking about emotionally charged topics. When they were ready for something that felt serious, they set the stage for an effective discussion by handling the three initial parts of the meeting well. They prevented a potential controversy from erupting during Chores by postponing further discussion of the concern until they reached the Problems and Challenges segment.

Lauren kept her communication positive and respectful, using I-statements and the sandwich approach. First she complimented Ken. Next she expressed her feeling of frustration. When Ken called her unfair, she avoided getting sidetracked by staying focused on her goal of improving teamwork. She made an I-statement to tell Ken exactly what she wanted from him and finished by complimenting him and expressing confidence that they would resolve the issue.

Let's backtrack for a moment. What if Ken had continued to refuse? Understanding that change takes time, Lauren would have raised her concern again at future meetings, using positive communication techniques. They might have brainstormed for solutions and agreed on one that fit both of them. For example, Ken might have been willing to try out a time-management system for a month. Or he might have been willing to use a system permanently if Lauren would have agreed to work on changing her lateness habit.

Although Ken had agreed to purchase a time-management system, what if he then forgot to do this? Lauren was prepared to be patient and to negotiate at their marriage meeting in a week by asking him, "If you haven't gotten it by next week's meeting, are you willing to tell me what kind you want and let me pick it up?"

Marriage Meetings Foster Growth in Both Partners

Ken did bring an appointment book with him to their next marriage meeting and made notes in it. Once he was using it regularly during their meetings, his reliability improved and Lauren's trust in him grew.

A FLEXIBLE ATTITUDE HELPS

For the sake of their relationship, Ken and Lauren both went outside of their comfort zones. For example, Lauren was flexible about the time and place to meet. Ken went along with the structured agenda for the meetings and then with the idea of using an appointment book.

Because each week's meeting reaffirms the value of their relationship, the couple has been able to keep minor annoyances in perspective and both partners are becoming willing to make changes from their usual way of being.

Ken used to agree to do things he would rather not do and then "forget" to do them. Now, instead of saying yes when he would rather say no, he is more likely to respond, "I'd rather not do that" or "I won't get to it for a few weeks." Lauren is glad. She likes to know the truth about how things stand. Ken still sometimes holds back on expressing disagreement. Lauren has learned to work around this when it happens. If she asks him if he's willing to handle a chore at home or to go somewhere with her, and he answers yes, but lukewarmly, Lauren might then ask, "Are you *really* willing to do that?" Sometimes she asks, "On a scale of one to ten how much do you want to do that?"

Lauren is also learning to distinguish between what is and what is not worth making an issue about. She knows that her perfectionism tempts her to focus too much on minor matters, like when she used to fret about Ken not wanting to buy her flowers. She tells herself that Ken is kind and generous in more important ways, that it would be nice, but not crucial, to get flowers. On the other hand, trust is important to her. She needs to be able to view her husband as someone who keeps agreements, which she can generally count on Ken to do. When he forgets to handle some minor matter, she tells herself to cut him some slack and that she's not perfect either.

Ken used to get angry at Lauren for calling him passive-aggressive when he forgot to do a chore. She has learned that name-calling makes things worse. Instead, she focuses on communicating positively. She is getting better at looking at the big picture, recognizing that while neither of them is perfect, she is fortunate to have a kind, loving husband she can relax with and laugh with, one who is there for her in the important ways.

In advance of their marriage meetings, Lauren often jots down things she notices Ken has done that she likes and consults her list during Appreciation. Once he hears what Lauren appreciates him for — such as for remembering to make an important phone call, for coming up with a great idea for a date, and for the good time they had in bed Saturday night — he is likely to want to please her in these ways in the future.

Ken and Lauren have succeeded, not by eliminating an "unresolvable" conflict born from their different natures, but in *managing* it, in learning to accept and adapt to each other. Ken remains a basically easygoing, laid-back type who is prone to ignore the details on which Lauren focuses.

Their weekly marriage meetings have helped them honor their differences and reconnect lovingly every week. They feel heard, supported, and cared for by each other. They are creating the marriage they've always wanted. Once again they are best friends and lovers.

CHAPTER  11

Resolving an In-law Issue

NED AND AMY

When a spouse is mistreated by an in-law, advisers commonly say that the partner who is related to the "abuser" should be the one to tell the relative politely but firmly to back off. But what if, for one reason or another, the partner does not take charge and instead allows the situation to continue? The story that follows shows how a couple used marriage meetings to help resolve such a challenge.

———— •◆• ————

The first time Amy met Ned's mother, it did not go well. Rhoda asked her, as they sat side by side on a couch in the living room of her in-laws-to-be, "How long have you lived in San Francisco?" Amy said, "Twelve years." Without missing a beat, Rhoda followed up with: "How old were you when you moved here from Minneapolis?" Ned and his mild-mannered father, Arnold, relaxing on nearby easy chairs, seemed not to notice Rhoda's transparent attempt to learn her age.

"She thinks she's being subtle!" Amy thought just before changing the subject. Amy, a few years older than Ned, was not about to give his mother ammunition she might use against her.

Yet once Ned and Amy got engaged, Rhoda welcomed her into

the family. She organized a bridal shower in a leafy, upscale neighborhood with large, landscaped lawns. Amy felt grateful to Rhoda for arranging the party in her honor.

IN-LAW CONFLICT BEGINS

On Amy and Ned's wedding day, soon after the ceremony, Rhoda told Amy that she looked heavy in her full-skirted wedding dress, borrowed from a friend. "If you'd bought a new dress, you would look better," she said.

When Amy made Thanksgiving dinner for her in-laws, Rhoda said her daughter's turkey was better. She tsk-tsked about the clutter on Amy's kitchen counter, which became an ongoing theme.

Amy tried to ignore Rhoda's put-downs. She invited her to brunch on the first Mother's Day after her marriage and again the next year. She wanted to be a good daughter-in-law.

When Ned and Amy's little girl, Ginny, became a toddler, Rhoda told Amy, "You're making a mistake telling her how great she is all the time. That's bad for her to think she's so special." When Ginny acted up, Rhoda said, "She's having a tantrum because she's copying you. You have to get your way all the time; she'll imitate you and become a tyrant." It went on and on.

WIFE WISHES HUSBAND WOULD SUPPORT HER

Ned would sit there and say nothing. Amy suspected he agreed with Rhoda's criticisms. When she said she wished he would defend her, Ned said he hadn't noticed any problem. "She puts me down left and right, criticizes my cooking and housekeeping, and implies that I'm not a good mother," Amy said. "You're usually there when it happens."

Ned said, "She likes you; she's just being helpful."

Amy thought, "He's still tied to his mother's apron strings."

Amy found excuses to avoid visiting her in-laws. She felt like a coward, but she was protecting herself. Sometimes she felt obliged to go. On one of these occasions, she decided that although she might need to take care of the situation herself, she would first give Ned one last chance to stand up for her.

By then Ned and Amy had held five marriage meetings, all of which went well. Following the guidelines for effective meetings, they had talked about what, for them, were easy-to-resolve challenges in early meetings, like whether to make Ginny's bedtime a bit later and about the pros and cons of keeping certain furnishings versus replacing them with new ones. Now felt like a good time for Amy to ask Ned again to support her when his mother criticized her.

Marriage Meeting Helps Couple Deal with Mother-in-Law Concern

Amy brought up the in-law issue during Problems and Challenges. All had gone well during Appreciation and Chores. When Amy was about to suggest a date for just the two of them during Plan for Good Times, Ned suggested that they visit his parents that Sunday. Amy felt a rush of adrenaline. That wasn't her idea of a good time. She took a few deep breaths to calm herself, then said she might go but she wanted to talk more about this during Problems and Challenges, because she had some feelings about it.

Ned wondered why she was making an issue out of a family visit. He said, "We haven't been there as a family in a couple of months. The last few times I asked you to go, you came up with an excuse."

Amy said, "That's true, but it's complicated for me. We're supposed to move emotionally charged topics to Problems and Challenges."

"Okay," Ned agreed. "But this is important to me. I can't keep putting them off each time they ask when we're coming. They want to see you. And I want to spend time with them with all of us there."

Amy said, "We'll definitely talk about it in a few minutes. Meanwhile, how about a date for just the two of us on Saturday night?" Ned said okay and she agreed to his movie suggestion.

During Problems and Challenges, Amy knew to be careful. She couldn't tell him that she felt as if his mother were a bee hovering around her, looking for a chance to sting. If she said that, he would say, "You're imagining that. She likes you."

Amy said, "I get upset when your mother criticizes me about my weight, my housekeeping, my cooking, and my shortcomings as a mother."

"She's just trying to make conversation," Ned said. "You're taking it too personally. She really likes you —"

"Excuse me, but I know when I'm being attacked."

"She's just trying to be helpful. Our visits mean a lot to her. I like to see my parents at least once a month. They're not getting any younger."

Amy took a couple of deep breaths. "I hear that you think Rhoda is trying to be helpful, that our visits mean a lot to her and also to you."

Feeling heard, Ned began to relax a little. "Yes, that's the gist of what I'm saying. It's been nearly two months since we've seen them. You keep making excuses."

Amy said, keeping her voice soft, "If I knew you'd have my back, I'd feel fine about going. But whenever I tell you how upset I am after she zings me, you say you didn't notice anything. I end up upset with you too for not helping me."

Mildly exasperated, Ned asked, "What do you want me to do?"

"I'd like you to stand up for me. Tell her you love clutter. Say you like a woman with meat on her bones. Tell her you think I'm a wonderful mother. Just say whatever will make her stop."

Ned said, his voice tired, "I still think it's all in your head, but

I'll try to notice and say something. Haven't we talked about this enough?"

"I hope you *will* notice and speak up for me. I appreciate your saying you'll try. Thank you." Amy took a deep breath and exhaled. "Okay, we'll go this Sunday and see how we do."

Amy would not necessarily be able to expect Ned to support her in Rhoda's presence, because "trying" isn't doing. Yet their conversation was successful because it included much positive communication and cleared the air, at least for the time being. Amy used I-statements. She also focused on nonverbal communication by keeping her voice tone soft and used the active listening technique, rephrasing a couple of comments Ned made, which helped him relax and feel understood.

The conversation brought some closure for Amy. She realized from Ned's less-than-wholehearted response that he was not likely to help. She could expect to be on her own Sunday. As stated in chapter 6, getting out of the martyr role in a marriage is a do-it-yourself job. She made a plan.

Sunday's visit began with the usual pleasantries. When the conversation lulled, Rhoda commented, looking toward Amy, "Ginny looks thin. You're making a big mistake by being so stubborn about not letting her eat cake and candy. Small children don't want fruit for dessert." Amy knew it would do no good to tell Rhoda that the doctor said Ginny is healthy.

Meanwhile, Ned and Arnold sat nearby, saying nothing.

Amy prided herself on keeping up with the latest nutritional findings. Still, you could never be sure, what with so much contradictory advice floating around. Sugar is fine for young children, sugar is bad for them, et cetera. Amy felt a twinge of doubt, quickly followed by resentment.

And what about Ned? How could he just sit there? Amy wondered. She wished he would say something like "We're the parents.

Right or wrong, we make the decisions." Rhoda would accept this from her son. Ned could even get away with joking, "You and Dad had your chance with me. Now it's our turn." Rhoda would smile, implying "I give in," maybe shrug her shoulders, and that would have been that. But no, Amy thought. Ned didn't have it in him to stand up to her. Nor would Arnold challenge Rhoda. Like father, like son. *So it's up to me.*

Amy Takes Action

"Excuse me," said Amy. She rose and headed to the bathroom. She looked in the mirror and took a few deep breaths. It's good to get away from them, she thought. She stayed there just long enough to feel calm, collected, and in charge of herself. After she returned to the living room, no one seemed to have noticed she'd been gone. Amy, too, acted blasé.

Her mini-revolt was a turning point. No longer would she feel the need to stick around when Rhoda got on her case.

Wife Uses Self-Talk Technique Effectively

On the way home, Amy felt annoyed with Ned for again failing to support her. She wanted to get over feeling this way and decided to use the self-talk technique. Here is how she put into practice its five steps, explained in chapter 8:

Step 1. *Be aware:* "What am I telling myself?"
   Amy recognizes she has been telling herself, "Ned is too weak to defend me. I wish he would change."
Step 2. *Evaluate:* "Is my self-talk helping?"
   She realizes her self-talk is destructive "because it's causing me to resent my husband and view him as inadequate."
Step 3. *Identify:* "What Driver, Stopper, or Confuser is operating to maintain my inner speech?"

Amy answers, "My Stopper is causing me to judge my husband as inadequate. My Driver is causing me to hold Ned to a perfectionistic standard he may not be able to reach because of his easygoing personality and his loyalty to his mother. My Confuser is mixing me up, causing me to view Ned negatively. It is making me overgeneralize. I am using black-and-white thinking instead of seeing the big picture, which includes his many excellent character traits."

Step 4. *Support yourself:* "What permission and self-affirmation will I give myself to replace my negative self-talk?" She tells herself, "I deserve respect. I have the right to take care of myself when Rhoda is disrespectful."

Step 5. *Develop your guide:* "What action will I take based on my new supportive position?"

Amy's action plan: "I will give all of us — my mother-in-law, my husband, and myself — permission to be ourselves. If I feel helpless and unsupported by Ned when Rhoda criticizes me, I will continue to take care of myself. As I did today, I can choose to leave the scene until I feel calm enough to rejoin the group and act as though nothing happened."

By the time Amy has finished her self-talk, she again appreciates her husband's fine qualities and accepts that she cannot expect him to help her deal with his mother. She realizes that she can manage her conflict with her mother-in-law while maintaining harmony between her husband and herself.

GAINING UNDERSTANDING

Once she had freed herself from feeling like her mother-in-law's victim, Amy wondered why it had taken her so long. Rhoda had an uncanny ability to tap into her insecurities. But even if her gibes had some truth to them, that wasn't really the point, was it? Rhoda had been out of line, and Amy had finally set a boundary.

Amy's perspective on Rhoda changed. Earlier, she had viewed Rhoda as an enemy. Now she realized that Rhoda, too, had insecurities. Possibly, thought Amy, her digs were attempts to even the score between herself and her younger, better educated daughter-in-law. Amy began to feel kinder toward Rhoda. She noticed things she liked about her, like how she stayed slim and dressed fashionably. Amy had lapsed into dressing for comfort in loose garments. She thought, "I like seeing people who dress well. I might want to shop for more flattering clothes." When she told Rhoda how good she looked in a new outfit and asked where she bought it, Rhoda almost blushed.

A MEETING OF THE MINDS

One evening, Amy confronted Rhoda directly, surprising them both. Amy and her friend Celia, who had come along for a visit, were speaking privately in the den. When Rhoda entered the room, Amy stopped speaking in midsentence. Rhoda looked hurt. Her eyes were teary as she asked Amy, "Why do you confide in her and not me?" Amy blurted out, "Because you criticize me so much."

That was the beginning of a meeting of the minds between Amy and her mother-in-law. They entered into a truce limiting their conversations to small talk. Each avoided saying anything that might stir up the other. When the climate felt safer, Rhoda actually became supportive. She told Amy that she was a good mother and that she made Ginny feel secure. When Rhoda occasionally slipped into criticizing, Amy gave her a look that said "back off" and she did. They developed an understanding that grew into a friendship.

MARRIAGE MEETINGS HELPED
A COUPLE GET PAST AN IMPASSE

Amy and Ned's story reveals that marriage meetings offer a supportive structure for resolving a long-standing issue. Their discussion during a meeting helped Amy gain closure regarding her husband's inability to help. Consequently, she realized that she would have to act on her own. Ned was relieved to be freed from the expectation that he should get involved in Amy's issue concerning his mother. Amy helped turn what had been an adversarial relationship with her mother-in-law into a supportive friendship. By using the marriage meeting tool and communication skills, she and her husband moved past an impasse and strengthened their relationship.

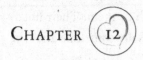

Handling a Money Conflict

SALLY AND MICHAEL

Money challenges are common in marriage. One of you might want to save for retirement, a house, or a child's education, and the other might like to spend more and live from paycheck to paycheck. One of you, not wanting to be in debt, may want to buy a used car for cash; the other may prefer to use that money as a down payment on a flashy new car and make payments for a few years. You may have different ideas about how much discretionary, "no questions asked," spending each of you should get to do.

Marriage meetings offer a structure for dealing with a wide range of concerns. Whether the issue is money or something else, the meeting provides a calm atmosphere for addressing differences by using positive communication skills. The story described here shows how a couple used marriage meetings to address a money issue.

———— • ◆ • ————

Michael and Sally, both forty, met in the high school where they taught math and English, respectively. Because of a large inheritance that legally would remain Michael's after marriage, according to their state's law, his assets far exceeded hers. When they were engaged, he had said, "I don't want a prenuptial agreement, because those marriages always end in divorce." They agreed to a joint checking account and separate ones for each of them. Their financial inequality developed into a concern for Sally sometime after she became a full-time mother.

COUPLE HOLDS MARRIAGE MEETINGS; MONEY ISSUE SURFACES

By then, Michael and Sally had been conducting marriage meetings for some time. After Sally stopped earning income, Michael dipped into his savings routinely to make ends meet. She often told him during the Appreciation part of their meetings that she was grateful to him for supporting the family.

After the birth of their second child, Sally began to feel uneasy about their different financial situations. Once she had quit her job, she was no longer able to save or invest. She felt vaguely uncomfortable about her husband being more financially secure than she. Michael was sharing some of his nest egg, but what if their marriage didn't last? He would still have plenty, and she would have virtually nothing.

Sally was confused by her feelings. Why couldn't she simply trust that he would always be there for her?

WIFE'S FAMILY BACKGROUND FUELS HER DOUBTS

Sally's parents had divorced when she was eleven. During her adolescence, she had heard her heartbroken mother lament more than once, "He left me after I gave him the best years of my life." Adding to Sally's insecurity was the knowledge that her mother's father had disappeared before her mother was born, leaving Sally's maternal grandmother destitute with two small children.

Sally wanted a "rainy day" fund. She felt ashamed to tell this to

Michael. It would be like admitting she thought their marriage might end, when he was so steadfast.

She wished she had as much faith as Michael showed in their union. She felt ashamed of wanting more money. She had learned at home as a child that to ask for it was greedy and selfish. Subconsciously, she believed this. Wasn't that what she would be doing by complaining about not having enough? Would Michael think she was a harpy?

SALLY BRINGS UP MONEY ISSUE IN MARRIAGE MEETINGS

With trepidation, Sally brought up her concern during the Problems and Challenges part of a marriage meeting. She told Michael she felt frustrated about being "one-down" financially in relation to him. He shrugged off her worry. He said he would always share his money with her. She tried again during another meeting, and again Michael seemed unconcerned.

She began to resent him for being insensitive. At the very least, she wanted to feel understood. He had put up a wall between them.

Sally could not tolerate being blocked for long. During another marriage meeting, she decided to try again, which she did during Problems and Challenges. They agreed to use the active listening technique described in chapter 9.

Sally began, "I'm feeling insecure about having no money going into my retirement account since I stopped earning income."

"I hear you saying you're feeling insecure about money," Michael said. "It bothers you that you're not putting money into your retirement account since you left your job. Did I get that right?"

"Yes, you did." Her voice shook as she said, "It's hard for me to talk about this. I'm feeling one-down in our relationship. You have much more money than I have, and that means you have more power than I do financially. It's more complicated than that though —"

"What do you want me to do? Give you half of my money?" he asked testily.

Sally, feeling accused of being greedy, said, "I don't expect that. I just know I'm uncomfortable. Your inheritance is legally all yours, but I gave up my job. It just doesn't feel okay for me to have no money coming in."

Michael sighed, exasperated.

Sally shook her head, discouraged. "I'm sorry I brought it up."

Did you notice when active listening stopped? Instead of reflecting back what he heard Sally say when she talked about their financial inequality, Michael reacted irritably. He feared he would have to part with a chunk of his inheritance. His own anxiety prevented him from hearing hers. When she tried to explain her feelings, he felt too threatened to take them in. Emotions ran too high on both sides to get the conversation back onto a positive track.

That night when Michael tried to hold her in bed, Sally pulled away. She was too upset to sleep. Michael felt confused and rejected.

Sally Changes Unhelpful Self-Talk into Constructive Messages

The next day Sally thought over what had happened. She told herself, "He's being selfish. He doesn't care about what happens to me. I could be left with nothing. I don't want to be another divorced woman who barely scrapes by because she expected her husband to stay."

Sally caught herself engaging in destructive self-talk. She decided to change this by using the five-step self-talk communication technique, as shown here:

Step 1. *Be aware:* "What am I telling myself?"

"I am telling myself that my husband is selfish and doesn't care what happens to me, that he might leave me and I'll be poor."

Step 2. *Evaluate:* "Is my self-talk helping?"

"My self-talk is not helping at all. It is upsetting me and making me distrust my husband."

Step 3. *Identify:* "What Driver, Stopper, or Confuser is operating to maintain my inner speech?"

"My 'be-perfect' Driver is saying that Michael should help resolve my money issue instead of being annoyed with me for bringing it up. My Stopper is saying that I should back off because I'm the selfish one and shouldn't be so insecure. My Confuser is causing me to fail to see the big picture. It is saying that my husband doesn't care about me."

Step 4. *Support yourself:* "What permission and self-affirmation will I give myself to replace my negative self-talk?"

"It is okay for me to recognize, respect, and act on my feelings. My feelings are as important as my husband's and deserve attention. It is worth taking the risk of sharing them with him. Michael often behaves in ways that show he cares for me."

Step 5. *Develop your guide:* "What action will I take based on my new supportive position?"

"Michael and I haven't yet finished the conversation. We need to hear each other out. The topic is very sensitive for each of us. I think we will do better by talking about it with a therapist present. I will suggest to Michael that we schedule a session."

Sally decided that during their next marriage meeting she would bring up the idea of their seeing a therapist together.

COUPLE MOVES TOWARD SOLUTION; THE MARRIAGE MEETING STRUCTURE HELPS

During the Appreciation part of their next marriage meeting, Sally again told Michael she was grateful to him for making it possible, through his financial support, for her to be home with their young children. She appreciated him also for making reservations for the play they saw Saturday night, for his consideration in letting her sleep the previous night when he got up to calm their crying baby, and for doing the kitchen cleanup so thoroughly every night after dinner.

Michael told Sally he appreciated her for taking the children to playgroup, for keeping herself stimulated intellectually by attending her book discussion group Tuesday night, for exercising with him at the gym Sunday, for her diligence in doing some research on the internet about a possible family trip to a national park, and for her consideration in listening to him talk about his frustration with on-the-job politics after he came home Monday.

As usually happens by the end of Appreciation, both partners were feeling good about each other. They handled the next two parts of their marriage meeting, Chores and Plan for Good Times, with ease.

When it was time for the last agenda topic, Problems and Challenges, Sally tried to smooth the discussion by using the communication technique for giving constructive criticism and feedback, which is explained in chapter 9.

First, she asked Michael, "Is it okay with you for us to talk more about my money issue?" Michael, looking less than thrilled, said okay. Then Sally used the "sandwich" approach:

Sally said, "It seems like we get stuck when I try to talk about our money situation. Are you willing to hear an idea I have that might help?"

Michael hesitated briefly and then said okay.

Sally began making the "sandwich" with a compliment. "I love you very much, so I want to clear the air between us. I am so grateful to you for taking care of all of us financially so that I can be a full-time mother while our children are young."

She next said, "I feel bad about how our conversation went last week when I said I felt one-down financially. It's hard for me to talk about money; and when you got upset with me, I felt intimidated and thought you didn't care about me. I'd like for us to get past this by talking it over together with a therapist."

Sally closed the "sandwich" by expressing positive feelings. "I know that you do care about me. It's my insecurity that makes me doubt it. You are really very generous with me in so many ways, so I know we'll feel better about each other once we have a healthy conversation about the subject."

Michael said, "Okay, but I don't want to be backed into a corner."

Sally said, "I don't want that either. I want a solution that works for both of us."

THE THERAPY SESSION

During their therapy session, Sally talked about the financial sacrifice she had made by choosing to become a full-time mother. She said, "I don't save anything, because I have no money coming in. Michael doesn't save either. He actually goes into his savings to keep us afloat. But he has a large nest egg, and I don't. I feel guilty for resenting this. Yet if anything happens to our marriage, it doesn't seem right that I would be left bereft financially and he would be fine."

Michael muttered something about men he heard about who got "cleaned out" by ex-wives.

Sally was taken aback and thought, "He doesn't trust me! Does he think I'm one of those scheming types? Is this really Michael?" She didn't know how to reconcile the Michael she knew with the one who had just spoken.

What happened to the trusting Michael who hadn't wanted a prenuptial agreement? Unlike Sally's parents, his were still happily married. Now it seemed that Michael, too, wanted to be prepared for any contingency, including the possibility that if worse came to worst, she would try to fleece him for all he was worth.

Sally realized, "He's feeling vulnerable, too." Why not? With close to one out of two marriages ending in divorce, statistics made marriage look like a gamble.

When the therapist asked Sally what she would like from Michael, she looked uncomfortable, because she felt guilty about asking for money. She swallowed, then said, "I'm working harder now than I ever did on a paid job, but I'm not getting a paycheck. It doesn't feel fair that because we decided I would stay home with our children that I should have to give up so much financially." She paused, then said, "I would like for Michael to contribute the same amount to my retirement account that was going into it when I was teaching."

Michael looked ill at ease. He closed his eyes briefly. Subconsciously, he was, in effect, completing the first four steps of the five-step self-talk communication technique. First, he thought, "I'm telling myself, 'Sally's taking me for a fool by expecting me to give her my money.'" Next, he recognized: "This message is not helping." Then he understood: "It is coming from my 'judge,' which is saying she is wrong to want me to share my money, and from my 'Confuser,' which is causing me not to see the whole picture."

Finally, he gave himself a more helpful message: "I've always liked Sally's sense of fairness. She is an ethical person from whom I have little to fear concerning money. By suspecting her of taking advantage of me, I've been making an *illogical inference*."

Michael relaxed as he realized, "Sally feels insecure. If our positions were reversed I'd probably feel that way too. She's working at home and taking good care of our children and spending more time doing this than I spend teaching. Meanwhile, I'm building a retirement account and she's not."

Having, in effect, completed the first four steps of the self-talk technique, Michael thought about what he would do. He wasn't ready to give Sally all of what she asked for because that felt like too much. Giving her only half of that amount didn't feel right either, because he would still have much more than she because of his largely untapped inheritance. He thought he should give her more than half of what she asked for. His response to Sally was step 5 of the self-talk technique, his action plan: "I'm willing to contribute two-thirds of the total amount you would be getting for retirement if you were teaching."

Sally exhaled with relief. She knew this was a stretch for Michael. She thanked him. "He's being generous," she thought, "even if it's not quite as much as I used to get. He cares enough to do this."

THE THERAPY SESSION PRODUCES CLOSURE

People generally find it hard to talk about feelings and needs about which they feel ashamed. We fear being judged by our partner if we are "too open." Even though their marriage felt secure, both Michael and Sally felt a need to be prepared, just in case. In the safety of a therapy session, they were able to reveal the truth they felt in their hearts.

Consequently, they gained understanding of and empathy for each other and arrived at a solution during the session. They left with more confidence in their ability to negotiate solutions to money and other concerns in the future.

Their story shows how marriage meetings can help a couple bring up a challenging issue, which, if left unattended, could result in grudge-building and other negative behaviors. It also shows how the meeting can help spouses know when it makes sense to consult a qualified therapist or other professional.

Sally and Michael used the marriage meeting tool and techniques to discuss a money issue calmly. They were wise to seek outside help. Each gained an understanding of the other's viewpoint during their therapy session, making it possible for them to create a happy ending.

Chapter 13

Couple Progresses from Verbal Abuse to Healthier Relating

Wendy and Zack

Not all couples are ready to hold successful marriage meetings, even during a therapy session. Although the spouses described in this chapter initially fell into this category, by using marriage meeting techniques during sessions they learned to communicate more positively. Their story also shows how a therapist can, by coaching a couple through a marriage meeting, quickly identify core issues to address during the course of treatment.

———— ◆ ————

Oh, no! I thought, on seeing the newspaper headline announcing my workshop: "Class for Couples with Problems." They shouldn't have done that. Marriage meetings are for basically healthy couples.

Although all couples experience problems, I feared that this headline would discourage well-functioning couples from attending. They would think the class was for people in seriously troubled relationships. So I wished they hadn't used the word *problems*.

Yet that word caught Zack's attention. He told his wife, Wendy, about me, and she phoned to request a private session for the two of them.

Couple Therapy Begins

As we got acquainted in my office, Wendy was soon sobbing. Married four years, they were experiencing *big* problems. "He calls me a slob," said Wendy.

Ignoring her sniffling, Zack countered, "She doesn't clean up after herself; she leaves her projects and newspapers all over the place."

I told them all relationships have ups and downs. "Thank you," Wendy said, sighing with relief. "Relationships are messy," I continued. "It's not like in the fairy tales, where you get to live happily ever after without having to put in effort. So it helps to get organized. Marriage meetings might help keep things on track between the two of you."

They liked the idea of having a structure, but they would need to repair their relationship before they could hold effective meetings. During their first attempts to hold marriage meetings in my office, one or the other of them would derail the agenda by blaming the other, interrupting, and using "colorful" language. They were not ready to follow the marriage meeting guideline calling for polite, respectful behavior. Each complained about the other's swearing; they agreed not to curse, but continued to let the four-letter words fly.

Wendy and Zack are recovering alcoholics, each with eight years of sobriety, which means they have proven that they can stay on course to achieve a goal.

Both grew up in troubled homes. Zack's alcoholic father often verbally abused him. Wendy's divorced mother brought home a series of boyfriends, one of whom sexually abused Wendy repeatedly during her teen years.

Wendy and Zack sabotaged nearly all of their early marriage meetings. During most sessions, the strong need each felt to vent about something the other said, did, or didn't do got in the way of their following the agenda.

Once, during Appreciation, Wendy gave Zack several heartfelt compliments. When it was his turn to reciprocate, he said sullenly, "I don't appreciate anything about her." Tears welled up in Wendy's eyes, and away they went into their "dance." Zack wasn't ready to use the self-control needed to put off dealing with an emotionally charged topic until the last part of the marriage meeting, Problems and Challenges.

During some sessions, Zack and Wendy would plan a date. They would agree to a day and time to take a walk, see a movie, or go out for dinner. A week later, Zack would come in frustrated because Wendy had come up with an excuse not to go.

Wendy said Zack embarrassed her by putting her down in front of her family members. He said he was just joking. She knew he wasn't.

A TURNING POINT FOR ZACK

After they had been seeing me for a few months, Zack's mother died. He came in with Wendy two days later, stunned and grief-stricken. When Wendy suggested that they do something "fun," my jaw nearly dropped. She meant well; she wanted to distract him. But that was the last thing he needed at the moment. Zack was showing his true feelings of deep sadness about a catastrophic loss; he needed to have them validated.

I told Wendy, "It's important to let Zack feel whatever he feels. He needs the time and space to grieve in his own way." Zack's eyes became teary. I think this was the first time he experienced the value of therapy as a place to express feelings other than anger.

Both partners seemed relieved to feel understood by me. Ideally, they would learn to provide that kind of acceptance to each other. Because neither Wendy nor Zack had ever seen a good marriage, they would also need to be educated about the practicalities of how to create one.

COMPLAINTS ABOUND; MARRIAGE EDUCATION BEGINS

In another session, during which Zack kept attacking Wendy verbally, I explained that an important element of a good relationship is the ability for partners to express disagreement respectfully. I showed them a chart I keep within easy reach in my office that lists five types of communication people use when disagreement exists (see pages 108–9).

I reviewed each mode, saving *congruent* for last. About congruent communication, Zack said, "That didn't happen in my family." Both he and Wendy recognized that they had grown up in an atmosphere with frequent blaming and placating, patterns they were repeating with each other.

By experimenting over time during therapy sessions and at home, they experienced the value of congruent communication. They realized that using I-statements showed respect for both themselves and each other.

PATIENCE IS A VIRTUE;
GLIMMERS OF HOPE ARE REWARDS

Wendy and Zack learned to be patient with the process of learning to communicate more effectively. It takes time to change a long-standing habit, and that change usually happens gradually, in baby steps.

In the meantime, glimmers of hope appeared. One of Zack's complaints had been that Wendy was "sloppy" and "careless." She thought he was obsessed with neatness. During a session in which they were able to complete a marriage meeting, they came up with a solution for this conflict. Zack was annoyed with Wendy for often letting things she was cooking boil over while she was elsewhere in their home. He criticized her for not cleaning up the spills promptly and thoroughly.

A Successful Marriage Meeting

During the first marriage meeting they completed, Wendy began to go off on a tangent during Appreciation, talking about something she wanted Zack to do to improve their relationship. He reminded her, "We need to stick to the agenda." During part 4 of this meeting, Problems and Challenges, they addressed their conflict about kitchen cleanliness. They agreed to my suggestion to use a communication technique explained in chapter 9, brainstorming for solutions.

They defined the challenge as "How can this couple live in harmony when Zack likes a clean kitchen and Wendy sometimes forgets to turn off the burner before what's cooking overflows?" They came up with a number of suggestions for solutions, which Wendy recorded. After the list was complete, we looked at each possibility. Wendy crossed out each one that either Zack or she rejected. Wendy turned down Zack's suggestion that she stay in the kitchen for the entire time the stove was on. Zack said no to her suggestion "Accept the situation and learn to live with it."

Then they evaluated the pros and cons of the other options. Finally they selected one they both agreed to: "When Wendy wants to leave the kitchen while cooking something on the stove, she will tell Zack and he will keep an eye on the situation and turn off the burner at the proper time."

This marriage meeting was successful for Wendy and Zack, first, because they followed the agenda, with Zack's help, and second, because they actually resolved an issue rather than simply venting about it.

Change Takes Time; Backsliding Happens

A week later Wendy said that Zack had again been cursing at her. Zack said she swore too. In another session, Zack kept attacking

Wendy verbally while the "Five Types of Communication People Use When Disagreement Exists" list (see pages 108–9) was in view. I told him, "You're blaming." He rose from the couch abruptly, seized his jacket, and rushed from the room, blurting out, "That's it! I'm done here!"

I was stunned. Had I just been too blunt? Was I blaming, too? Was he never coming back? These thoughts raced through my head. Wendy seemed untroubled. "I think this is a breakthrough," she said, apparently sensing that Zack's behavior meant I had reached him. I realized that he had felt criticized by me and reacted by hiding his hurt in a cloud of anger.

COUPLE REPORTS PROGRESS
BEFORE BACKSLIDING AGAIN

During the next session, they reported progress. They had expressed appreciation during the week both verbally and by writing notes to each other. Wendy told Zack that she wanted massages from him without the expectation of sexual intercourse. Zack looked uncomfortable and the subject was not pursued. However, she had done well in phrasing what she wanted as a desire rather than as a complaint.

LACK OF EMPATHY IS A MAJOR OBSTACLE

But a week later Wendy was criticizing Zack for being a down-to-earth kind of guy. She said she likes a more intellectual type of man.

Because they showed so little empathy for each other, I began to wonder whether couple therapy was the best way for them to improve their relationship. After six months of weekly sessions, I had perceived little change in their relationship. Sometimes while Wendy talked about a delicate subject with tears in her eyes, Zack would look up at the ceiling and roll his eyes or maintain a blank expression. He seemed unable to tolerate her expressions of vulnerability.

Emotional intimacy requires that partners feel safe enough to express their feelings openly with each other. Zack and Wendy's difficulty in accepting each other's vulnerability convinced me that they needed more than marriage meetings and couple therapy to feel an ongoing sense of emotional connection. Neither partner had a reservoir of empathy to draw from in order to tune in to each other's tender emotions.

I realized that before they would be able to respond supportively to each other, each would need to gain self-empathy.

INDIVIDUAL THERAPY FOR EACH SPOUSE

"Before each of you can have compassion for the other," I said, "you need to gain compassion for yourselves." I recommended that they receive individual therapy. We agreed to discontinue weekly couple sessions, with the understanding that these could still be scheduled by their request or mine.

Interestingly, both expressed sadness about ending ongoing couple therapy. They said, "It's the only time we talk." For them, "talking" apparently meant being able to air resentments. But they also agreed to individual therapy, Zack with me and Wendy with a different therapist.[1]

ZACK SIGNS ON

During Zack's first individual session, I drew a sketch of an iceberg to explain how feelings below the surface, meaning those we are not aware of, influence how we speak and behave, for better or worse.

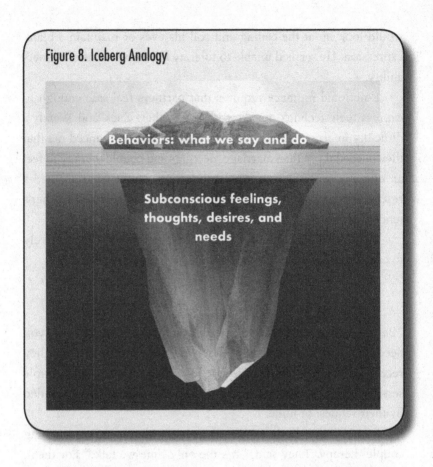

Figure 8. Iceberg Analogy

Behaviors: what we say and do

Subconscious feelings, thoughts, desires, and needs

Soon Zack began to pay more attention to his feelings and to use I-statements to express them. He later reported that, instead of belittling Wendy for being late, he had said, "When you're late for going out to a movie with me, I feel hurt." He also related that, when he spoke to Wendy this way, she had "been understanding."

MARRIAGE MEETING SKILLS ENHANCE THE RELATIONSHIP

More positive changes followed. Zack and Wendy started leaving appreciative notes for each other more often. Cursing became less of an issue because they had set up a "cuss box" into which whoever swore would have to put a dollar.

Zack eased the housekeeping conflict by arranging for a house-cleaner to come in regularly. He complained about how quickly Wendy let things deteriorate, but his tone was accepting, as though he were saying, "This is as good as it will get." They were learning to live and let live.

Near the end of his individual therapy, Zack was scheduled for an operation, to be followed by a week of bed rest. After a similar procedure a year earlier, he had been disappointed with Wendy for not having been around to help him much. Now he told her, "The last time this happened, I felt you weren't there for me." She promptly arranged to take a week off from work to be with him.

Zack and Wendy's relationship improved because they learned to use communication skills prescribed for marriage meetings. They developed new habits. They used I-statements often to express their feelings, wants, and needs. They gave each other frequent doses of appreciation. Instead of disengaging when the other expressed vulnerability, they became better at listening empathically. As both of them increased in self-understanding and self-acceptance, they learned to communicate authentically, creating a more trusting and meaningful relationship.

Marriage Meetings Enhance Therapy

Zack and Wendy's marriage meetings during their couple therapy sessions revealed some of their communication strengths and weaknesses. The structure and guidelines of the meetings introduced them to positive communication skills that they began to use every day. Their example shows how even couples with seemingly daunting challenges can benefit from holding marriage meetings in a supportive therapy environment.

CHAPTER  14

Marriage Meeting Techniques Support Couple Therapy

OLIVER AND ROBIN

This couple's story shows how marriage meeting techniques, when integrated into therapy sessions, can help restore even a severely damaged relationship. Their marriage meetings served as a diagnostic tool, uncovering key issues. These spouses were also introduced to and benefited from using positive communication skills.

———— • ◆ • ————

Oliver and Robin look like a beautiful couple who could star in a television commercial. Tall and well built, with blue eyes and a tanned complexion, Oliver is an emergency room physician. Robin, an occupational therapist, is a slim, petite redhead with a peaches-and-cream complexion and bright smile. Both in their late thirties and married sixteen years, they have three children who are apparently doing exceptionally well in elementary school.

This couple's relationship has included physical violence, infidelity, and alcoholism, any one of which is commonly said to cause divorce. However, despite their challenges, this couple expressed a commitment to rebuild their marriage.

Robin said that, before they began couple therapy, their usual way of handling disagreements was "to have screaming fights."

Sometimes when he was angry, Oliver would punch a door with his fist, making a hole. Often his rage was triggered by his wife's refusal to respond to his sexual advances. When he began to suspect her of infidelity, their arguments became physical.

Robin had begun having affairs a few years earlier. When Oliver found out, she promised to stop, but she did not and lied to him about her activities. When he discovered the truth, he beat her up. Drunk at the time, he bruised her body all over and struck her face hard enough to cause bleeding. This time she called the police, which she had not done before.

Couple Seeks to Repair Their Relationship

Oliver persuaded Robin to stay with him to try to work things out. He vowed, "I'll never touch another drop of alcohol again" and joined a support group for men who had abused their partners physically.

During their first therapy session with me, Oliver said, "Hopefully we can learn to communicate without yelling and screaming. I want to rebuild the trust that's been lost between us. This is my last chance to save my marriage." Robin said, "I want to be less indifferent to my husband, to care more about him." She said she didn't want a divorce; she wanted their children to grow up in an intact family.

Seeds for Current Challenges Planted in Childhood

As is typical of many people who are violent, Oliver was repeating what he had learned early in life. As a child he was beaten often by his father, who had also been physically violent toward Oliver's mother in his presence.

Robin's alcoholic father died when she was a year old. Because her mother was clinically depressed, Robin and her siblings had to fend for themselves, and "no one talked about feelings."

In Early Sessions, the Husband Is Controlling and the Wife Is Passive

During their early sessions I was struck by how Oliver kept speaking for Robin as though he needed to control her. Her bland facial expression suggested that this was nothing new. I told Oliver that I would like to hear what Robin wanted to say in her own words. Robin said her infidelity was "a symptom of what was wrong with the relationship," and that before her affairs began she and Oliver had been relating destructively for some time. Regarding her unfaithfulness, Oliver was teary as he said, "It just breaks me up."

Robin spoke about the frequent "forced sex" she had endured with Oliver for a couple of years, which had been physically and emotionally painful. Oliver said he had been upset for a long time, and "she always calls me stupid." When I asked Robin, "What would get the loving feelings back?" she said, "Dealing with conflict respectfully." I couldn't have said it better.

Therapist Demonstrates Self-Talk Communication Skill

About Oliver's physical violence toward her, Robin said during their second therapy session, "I can't believe he would treat me that way if he loves me." Although Robin and Oliver's relationship was not yet healthy enough for them to hold a marriage meeting, she was receptive to learning the self-talk communication technique, which is explained in chapter 8.

We began the self-talk exercise with Robin's statement "I can't believe he would treat me that way if he loves me." On a white-board, I listed each of the five steps of the self-talk technique. Robin's responses to the questions asked at each step are shown here, along with my suggestions:

Step 1. *Be aware:* "What am I telling myself?"

"I don't believe he loves me. If he did, he would never treat me that way."

Step 2. *Evaluate:* "Is my self-talk helping? (Is it supportive or destructive?)"

"It is not supportive."

Step 3. *Identify:* "What Driver, Stopper, or Confuser is operating?"

After I explained these concepts to Robin, she was able to realize: "My self-talk comes from my Confuser, which is causing me to conclude something is true when it may not be. I am *assuming* that my husband's violent behavior means he doesn't love me."

Step 4. *Support yourself:* "What permission and self-affirmation will I give myself?"

To help Robin replace her negative self-talk with a more helpful message, I recommended that she tell herself, "Oliver acts that way because he is afraid of losing me." I sensed from her surprised expression that she was taking in the possibility that Oliver's violence, devastating as it was for her, was his desperate attempt to hold on to her.

Step 5. *Develop your guide:* "What action will I take based on my new supportive position?"

Demonstrating this final step of the self-talk technique, I suggested that she decide: "I will take any action needed to protect myself and take care of myself as best I can, including calling the police."

Robin sounded pleased when she said, "I never thought of it that way," regarding the idea of viewing his violence as his drastic way of trying to keep her with him. I think she felt validated for having called the police after Oliver's recent violence.

Couple Tries Out Part 1
·of the Marriage Meeting: Appreciation

In their fourth therapy session, when it was clear that Robin and Oliver felt comfortable with the structure, communication, and education our sessions provided, I told them briefly about marriage meetings. As with many couples who come for therapy, the concept appealed to them because it offered what had been missing from their lives: a structure and directions for healthy communicating.

Starting gradually, I suggested that they hold the first part of a marriage meeting, Appreciation, and explained how to use I-statements to express appreciation. I advised them to include details, such as by specifying when and where the appreciated behavior occurred.

I asked Robin, the less verbal partner, to go first. Her first appreciative comments were "I appreciate you for building a bookcase for me," and "I appreciate how playful you were with the kids."

Oliver's compliments to Robin flowed easily. They included "I appreciate your suggesting we have lunch together on Wednesday" and "I appreciate how beautiful you are."

Given that this was their first try, I was satisfied. I did not ask Robin to say *when* or *how* Oliver had been playful with the kids. Nor did I tell Oliver to be more specific with his last compliment, which was global. My only suggestion was to remember to use I-statements, because I wanted them to feel encouraged at this stage. We could work on refining their appreciative comments in the future.

After six sessions, Oliver and Robin agreed their relationship was improving.

Oliver and Robin Try a Marriage Meeting

This seemed like a good time to try a marriage meeting with them. Walking them through it helped to identify a core relationship challenge.

During Appreciation, this time I encouraged them to be specific and to try naming a character trait that the behavior revealed, as in "I appreciate your *thoughtfulness* in picking up a take-out lunch for us to eat *in the park last Thursday*."

They conducted the Chores part of the meeting easily, agreeing on who would drive their oldest child home from an after-school event that Monday.

Part 3 of the Marriage Meeting Reveals a Challenge

When it was time for Plan for Good Times, the third part of a marriage meeting, I reminded them that this was the time to plan a date for the two of them.

"I have an idea," said Robin, surprisingly animated. "Let's take the kids to the zoo on Sunday."

When I asked Robin if she might be willing to make and keep a date for just the two of them, she talked about how little free time there was and the importance of doing fun things as a family. Oliver's face showed his disappointment.

A Sensitive Topic Gets Moved to Part 4 of the Marriage Meeting

Obviously, we had hit on a touchy topic. The structure of the marriage meeting puts discussion about highly sensitive issues in the fourth part of the marriage meeting, Problems and Challenges. Generally, such emotionally charged concerns should not be brought up until after a couple holds at least four to six successful meetings. However, this rule can be bent for meetings that occur with a therapist present.

When I told Oliver and Robin that dates for just the two of them appeared to be too complicated a topic for this part of their marriage meeting, they agreed to move that topic to Problems and Challenges.

When we returned to the subject, I asked Robin, "Does your hesitation to make a date for just the two of you have something to do with expectations?" She nodded. "He expects a date to be romantic. Romance should be spontaneous." She clarified that by *romantic*, she meant that Oliver expected them to have sexual relations after a date and said she didn't like feeling pressured.

Oliver spoke up. "When is the last time I had expectations?" She agreed that it had been a while.

"So it's not coming from me; it's your issue," Oliver said.

Robin then agreed to a dinner date with him, perhaps feeling obliged to do so at the moment.

How the Marriage Meeting Improved Communication

I believe the marriage meeting made it possible for this couple to focus on an issue that was causing tension because they had been dealing with it indirectly. Robin had been avoiding going on dates with Oliver without explaining why. He was feeling frustrated about this but not telling her.

Oliver and Robin reported a week after their marriage meeting that this time they did go on the date they had planned during the meeting. When they returned home they spent time with their children. Oliver had kept his end of the bargain. He had not pressed her for "romance," but he looked sad while reporting this.

Another time, Robin agreed to go on a dinner date with Oliver, but when they were about to leave she asked him to do shopping errands with her instead. He said he would, although he was not happy about the changed plan.

It will take time for Oliver and Robin to regain trust in each other and to learn to communicate and respect each other as equal partners.

Oliver is not yet able to empathize with Robin's state of mind.

He views romance and sex with Robin as proof that she loves him. She cannot give him this now. Robin is numb. For her, this is her way of keeping herself from being vulnerable with him after all of his violence and after years of experiencing his attempts to control her. When he asks her for hugs, she tells him, "You're too clingy."

Serious Conflicts Continue

Two major complications exist for this couple. First, Robin continues to feel emotionally distant from Oliver. He had beaten her up just a couple of weeks before they began couple therapy. There had been prior incidents, but the last one had been the most violent. Robin has a huge backlog of resentment. "He forced me to have sex with him every other night," she said. "I was afraid to refuse, because if I said no he would yell and throw things at me. If we lived in a third-world country where a husband could kill his wife, I believe he would have killed me."

Oliver understands that it is logical that Robin would not want physical intimacy with him. But he is still in denial emotionally. He wants to whitewash the past immediately and live happily ever after.

The Challenge of Restoring Trust

According to infidelity specialist Bill Herring, LCSW, "Significant negative impact of infidelity can be evident for anywhere between nine months to two years, while more complete healing often requires a much longer period of time."[1] It seems safe to assume that restoring the relationship after domestic violence would also be a lengthy process. Trust takes time. Oliver has heard this, but he does not want to wait. He still tries to force sexual intimacy. He then apologizes to Robin profusely. She has told him, "It's okay. Give it time."

In the meantime, their challenge is to respect and accept each other's differences. They still try to dominate each other at times by using you-statements instead of allowing themselves to be emotionally vulnerable by using I-statements to express their true feelings, wants, and needs.

Oliver says, "I wish we would have marriage meetings." Robin says, "He thinks that if we do that, it will fix everything between us." Her perception is probably accurate. Oliver wants an end to the distress he says he feels every day. He fears that his wife will never love him again.

What Robin said about giving it time is right. Time is their main ally, or is likely to be, as long as they continue to work on improving their relationship.

BRAINSTORMING FOR SOLUTIONS GENERATES IDEAS FOR BETTER RELATING

Robin and Oliver are experiencing an impasse. He continues to press her for signs that she loves him, which she is not able to provide. She needs time and space to heal. So she pulls away, which results in his feeling more desperate for affection from her and sex with her, creating a vicious cycle because his efforts to gain proof that she loves him push her further away. They agreed to my suggestion that they try to address this challenge with the brainstorming for solutions communication technique.

I reviewed the basic rules for brainstorming, explaining that the first step is to define the challenge or problem in a way that respects both of them. The next step is to list all ideas for solutions, including zany unexpected ones, without judging any of them.

Robin and Oliver agreed to define the challenge as "How can Robin and Oliver live in harmony when Robin needs physical and emotional distance from Oliver and Oliver craves reassurance, verbally and physically — including sexually — that Robin loves him?"

Following the instructions for brainstorming, the three of us contributed ideas, refraining from evaluating any of them before completing this list:

1. Robin agrees to have sex with Oliver. (Oliver says, only half-joking)
2. Oliver agrees to wait for Robin to initiate any physical contact. (Robin)
3. Recognize that Robin needs time to heal and to learn to trust Oliver to respect her autonomy. (me)
4. Recognize that Oliver needs time to heal before he will trust Robin to be faithful. (me)
5. Oliver and Robin decide to relate as platonic friends until both feel ready for more intimacy. (me)
6. Oliver makes plans to spend time with his own friends. (Oliver)
7. Lie to each other. (me, with irony)
8. Robin and Oliver read about how couples repair their marriage after an affair and after domestic violence. (me)
9. Have a referee move into their home. (me, wryly)
10. Robin gains support by participating in a group for abused women. (Oliver)
11. Oliver continues to participate in his men's domestic abuse group. (Oliver)

Next, each suggestion that one or both spouses vetoed got crossed out. The spouse who rejected an idea is identified in this altered list:

1. ~~Robin agrees to have sex with Oliver.~~ (Robin vetoed)
2. ~~Oliver agrees to wait for Robin to initiate any physical contact.~~ (Oliver vetoed)
3. Recognize that Robin needs time to heal and to learn to trust Oliver to respect her autonomy.

4. Recognize that Oliver needs time to heal before he will trust Robin to be faithful.
5. Oliver and Robin decide to relate as platonic friends until both feel ready for more intimacy.
6. Oliver makes plans to spend time with his own friends.
7. ~~Lie to each other.~~ (Robin and Oliver vetoed)
8. Robin and Oliver read about how couples repair their marriage after an affair and after domestic violence.
9. ~~Have a referee move into their home.~~ (Robin and Oliver vetoed)
10. Robin gains support by participating in group for abused women.
11. Oliver continues to participate in his men's domestic abuse group.

Following is the list of the seven potential solutions that both Robin and Oliver agreed to consider acting upon:

1. Recognize that Robin needs time to heal and to learn to trust Oliver to respect her autonomy.
2. Recognize that Oliver needs time to heal before he will trust Robin to be faithful.
3. Oliver and Robin decide to relate as platonic friends until both feel ready for more intimacy.
4. Oliver makes plans to spend time with his own friends.
5. Robin and Oliver read about how couples repair their marriage after an affair and after domestic violence.
6. Robin gains support by participating in a group for abused women.
7. Oliver continues to participate in his men's domestic abuse group.

MOVING PAST THE IMPASSE

For a couple that had been deadlocked when beginning this exercise to agree on seven ideas to consider is no small thing. The next step was for them to choose which idea(s) they were ready to implement. Both agreed to begin with number 3 on the final list of possible solutions: "Oliver and Robin decide to relate as platonic friends until both feel ready for more intimacy."

The six other ideas remaining on the list are topics Oliver and Robin can continue to discuss during therapy sessions and on their own. It is a good sign that Oliver is open to the idea of spending more time with friends. Socializing with others could help him be less "clingy" toward Robin, as she puts it, and make it easier for him to give her the space she craves.

It takes a leap of faith for anyone to get married. Robin and Oliver will each need to take another one to restore their marriage. She will need to trust him to treat her as a separate person with her own wants and needs rather than as someone he can control. He will have to trust that she will be faithful to him from now on. But first he will probably need to prove that he accepts her independence and not try to force himself on her sexually when she is not interested.

Oliver and Robin are learning to communicate more positively. Sometimes they catch themselves and each other giving blaming you-statement-type messages and shift to congruent communication by making I-statements. Recently, Robin told Oliver that his way of doing something was "wrong." He responded, "I think it is okay for us to be different." Little by little, they are learning to "attack the problem, not each other." Robin is slowly becoming more comfortable expressing herself more directly. Therapy is continuing to help both of them gain self-understanding, feel supported and validated, and become somewhat more attuned to each other. So far, so good.

Like this couple, most who enter therapy will need to be coached through the marriage meeting process, step-by-step, in order to hold an effective meeting. Otherwise, their issues are likely to get in the way of adhering to the marriage meeting's guidelines and agenda, and they will forget to use positive communication techniques.

In a recent session, I asked Robin and Oliver whether they would like to be able to hold marriage meetings on their own eventually. "I would love that," said Robin. Oliver added, "That would be awesome."

Conclusion

Children who grow up in a home with marital harmony are likely to learn, as if by osmosis, how to create a fulfilling marriage. They go on to set a similar example for their own children. Because they have gleaned how to communicate respectfully and positively, they are likely to have satisfying relationships with their life partners and with other people.

However, if this was not your experience as a child, you have all the more reason to want to learn skills to gain and keep a good marriage.

Whether or not you are married and whether or not you have children, even without holding formal marriage meetings you can increase your ability to create happier interactions. By putting into practice even one of the positive communication skills explained in chapters 7, 8, and 9, or by freeing yourself from even one of the marriage myths described in chapter 2, you will relate more joyfully to others. And you will be improving the world.

"The whole world?" I imagine you thinking incredulously. "Just because I use an I-statement when talking to my wife, husband, partner, child, friend, colleague, or coworker, I'll be changing the world?"

Yes, the whole world! Every action we take has a ripple effect. Picture yourself dropping a pebble into a lake. See the little wave it makes, a circular one that surrounds the place where the stone entered the water. Watch the wave move farther and farther out from that spot. By engaging in one small action that seems minor in the grand scheme of things, such as when you give a compliment, really listen, change destructive self-talk to constructive messages, communicate clearly, and so on, you are forming little waves that influence the universe in ways you cannot imagine.

When all is said and done, the art of marriage is really the art of keeping up to date with your partner, of staying on track with your own and each other's life goals as they emerge, exist, and change. It is about supporting each other and staying connected emotionally, intellectually, physically, and spiritually.

The Marriage Meeting Program is elegantly simple:

- Meet every week.
- Follow the recommended guidelines and agenda for your meetings.
- Use positive communication skills.

Allow yourselves time to get used to the formal structure of the meetings and to talking to each other in new ways. You may feel self-conscious at the beginning. This is normal. Give yourself credit for being disciplined enough to continue with the program as you gain skills and comfort in using the tools, techniques, and tips offered in this book.

Effective marriage meetings foster intimacy, romance, teamwork, and the smoother resolution of conflicts.

It is time to schedule your first meeting. It should go well. You are on your way to creating the marriage you've always wanted!

APPENDIX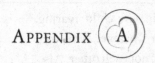

The Marriage Meeting Agenda
A QUICK-REFERENCE GUIDE

1. **Appreciation**

   Each spouse takes a turn giving a list of compliments to the other. Start each sentence with "I appreciate" or "I like." The other person listens without interrupting and then says thank you.

   Hints: Be specific, point out the good character traits (for example, reliability, responsibility, considerateness, kindness, sensitivity, and so on) that your partner has demonstrated by means of specific behaviors. Ask, "Did I leave anything out?"

2. **Chores**

   Each partner mentions tasks that need to be taken care of and reports on chores in progress. Agree on priorities and on who will do what, and when. Keep the focus positive.

3. **Plan for Good Times**

   Plan for "quality time" together and for family outings and vacations. Spouses may also plan activities they do individually. Know yourself and what it takes to recharge your batteries and keep your relationship energized.

4. **Problems and Challenges**
   The issues may involve money, intimacy, child rearing, education, relatives, life transitions, or whatever is on your mind. Remember: Attack the problem, not each other. Also, in early meetings bring up only easy-to-resolve concerns. Use I-statements, self-talk, congruent communication, active listening, nonverbal messages, constructive criticism and feedback, and brainstorming for solutions. Be patient, and stay with the process. You are likely to resolve many issues right away; others will take longer. Be willing to postpone some discussions.

Notes

- If discussion becomes too emotionally charged or argumentative during one of the three earlier parts of the meeting, move that conversation to part 4, Problems and Challenges.
- Schedule the next marriage meeting before the current meeting ends — for example, during Chores — unless you have already established a consistent meeting day and time each week.
- End on a positive note. Thank each other for meeting. Do something enjoyable afterward, either alone or together.
- You are welcome to reproduce these agenda instructions for your personal use.

© Marcia Naomi Berger, LCSW

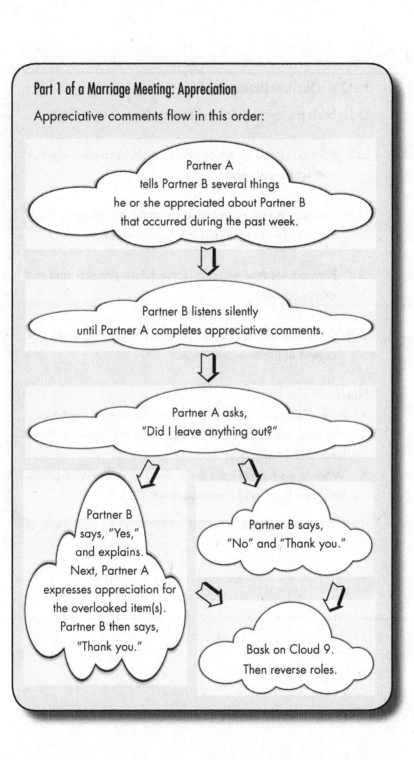

Part 1 of a Marriage Meeting: Appreciation

Appreciative comments flow in this order:

Partner A tells Partner B several things he or she appreciated about Partner B that occurred during the past week.

Partner B listens silently until Partner A completes appreciative comments.

Partner A asks, "Did I leave anything out?"

Partner B says, "Yes," and explains. Next, Partner A expresses appreciation for the overlooked item(s). Partner B then says, "Thank you."

Partner B says, "No" and "Thank you."

Bask on Cloud 9. Then reverse roles.

Part 2 of a Marriage Meeting: Chores

☐ 1. Each partner mentions chores on his or her to-do list.

☐ 2. Partners agree on which chores to do or begin this week and which can wait.

☐ 3. Partners agree on who will handle or delegate each chore to be done during the coming week.

☐ 4. Partners set time lines for some future projects and put others on hold.

☐ 5. Each partner reports on progress regarding tasks discussed in previous meetings.

Notes:
- If a discussion about a chore becomes emotionally charged, move that topic to part 4 of the meeting, Problems and Challenges.
- When the situation calls for it, be willing to revise priorities, time lines, and responsibilities.

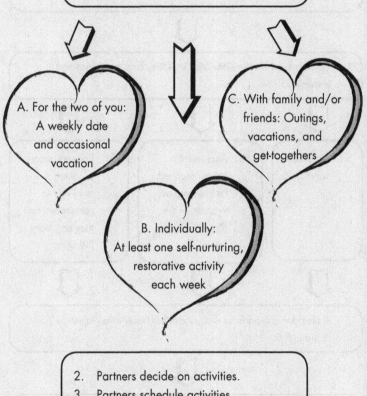

Part 3 of a Marriage Meeting: Plan for Good Times

1. Partners present ideas for enjoyable activities, using I-statements, active listening, and brainstorming to generate ideas.

A. For the two of you: A weekly date and occasional vacation

B. Individually: At least one self-nurturing, restorative activity each week

C. With family and/or friends: Outings, vacations, and get-togethers

2. Partners decide on activities.
3. Partners schedule activities.

Note: If a discussion about an activity becomes heated, move that topic to part 4 of the meeting, Problems and Challenges.

Part 4 of a Marriage Meeting: Problems and Challenges

1. Partner A, using I-statements, mentions an area of concern to be discussed.
2. Partner B responds using active listening skills.
3. Once partner A feels understood by B, partner B expresses his or her thoughts and feelings about the subject, while partner A listens actively.

4. Partners continue the discussion until they both feel heard and understood.

5a. Agreement is reached.	5b. Agreement is not yet reached. Partners agree to continue the discussion in the future.	5c. Partners accept problems that are likely to remain and that they can learn to live with.

6. If time permits, partners discuss another issue, following steps 1 through 5.

7. Partners conclude the meeting on a positive note, thanking each other for participating.

Note: In early marriage meetings, address only easy-to-resolve problems and challenges. Establish a pattern of successful meetings before trying to resolve a serious relationship issue.

The Feelings Inventories and Needs Inventory

The inventories in this appendix, included with permission from the Center for Nonviolent Communication, are meant to assist you in recognizing emotional states and needs in yourself that human beings experience. Both in marriage meetings and in everyday life, using I-statements to express your feelings, wants, and needs will foster positive and productive discussions.

THE FEELINGS INVENTORIES

There are two parts to the "Feelings" list: feelings we may have when our needs are being met, and feelings we may have when our needs are not being met.

Feelings Inventory — When Your Needs *Are* Satisfied

Affectionate	tender	curious
compassionate	warm	enchanted
friendly		engrossed
loving	**Engaged**	entranced
openhearted	absorbed	fascinated
sympathetic	alert	interested

intrigued
involved
spellbound
stimulated

Hopeful
encouraged
expectant
optimistic

Confident
empowered
open
proud
safe
secure

Excited
amazed
animated
ardent
aroused
astonished
dazzled
eager
energetic
enthusiastic
giddy
invigorated
lively
passionate

surprised
vibrant

Grateful
appreciative
moved
thankful
touched

Inspired
amazed
awed
wonder

Joyful
amused
delighted
glad
happy
jubilant
pleased
tickled

Exhilarated
blissful
ecstatic
elated
enthralled
exuberant
radiant

rapturous
thrilled

Peaceful
calm
centered
clearheaded
comfortable
content
equanimous
fulfilled
mellow
quiet
relaxed
relieved
satisfied
serene
still
tranquil
trusting

Refreshed
enlivened
rejuvenated
renewed
rested
restored
revived

Feelings Inventory — When Your Needs *Are Not* Satisfied

Afraid
apprehensive
dread
foreboding
frightened
mistrustful
panicked
petrified
scared
suspicious
terrified
wary
worried

Angry
enraged
furious
incensed
indignant
irate
livid
outraged
resentful

Annoyed
aggravated
disgruntled
dismayed
displeased
exasperated
frustrated

impatient
irked
irritated

Aversion
animosity
appalled
contempt
disgusted
dislike
hate
horrified
hostile
repulsed

Confused
ambivalent
baffled
bewildered
dazed
hesitant
lost
mystified
perplexed
puzzled
torn

Disconnected
alienated
aloof
apathetic

bored
cold
detached
distant
distracted
indifferent
numb
removed
uninterested
withdrawn

Disquiet
agitated
alarmed
discombobulated
disconcerted
disturbed
perturbed
rattled
restless
shocked
startled
surprised
troubled
turbulent
turmoil
uncomfortable
uneasy
unnerved
unsettled
upset

Embarrassed
ashamed
chagrined
flustered
guilty
mortified
self-conscious

Fatigue
beat
burnt out
depleted
exhausted
lethargic
listless
sleepy

tired
weary
worn out

Pain
agony
anguished
bereaved
devastated
grief
heartbroken
hurt
lonely
miserable
regretful
remorseful

Sad
dejected
depressed
despair
despondent
disappointed
discouraged
disheartened
forlorn
gloomy
heavy hearted
hopeless
melancholy
unhappy
wretched

The Needs Inventory

The following list of needs is neither exhaustive nor definitive. It is meant as a starting place to support anyone who wishes to engage in a process of deepening self-discovery and to facilitate greater understanding and connection between people.

Connection
acceptance
affection
appreciation
belonging
closeness
communication
community
companionship

compassion
consideration
consistency
cooperation
empathy
inclusion
intimacy
love
mutuality

nurturing
respect/self-respect
safety
security
stability
support
to know and be
    known
to see and be seen

to understand and
be understood
trust
warmth

**Physical
Well-Being**
air
food
movement/exercise
rest/sleep
safety
sexual expression
shelter
touch
water

Honesty
authenticity
integrity
presence

Play
humor
joy

Peace
beauty
communion
ease
equality
harmony
inspiration
order

Autonomy
choice
freedom
independence
space
spontaneity

Meaning
awareness
celebration of life
challenge
clarity
competence
consciousness
contribution
creativity
discovery
effectiveness
efficacy
growth
hope
learning
mourning
participation
purpose
self-expression
stimulation
to matter
understanding

Acknowledgments

Writing is a deeply rewarding yet solitary occupation with work-related hazards: loneliness and lack of feedback. Fortunately, antidotes exist. Writers' communities, friends, colleagues, and family sustain and inspire me.

I treasure past and present writing critique group members Judith Bolinger; Robert Evans; Lynn Fraley, PhD; Leslie Marks; Judith Marshall; Sylvia Mills, PhD; Teresa LeYung Ryan; Lynn Scott; Jeff Stoffer; Diane Vickers; and Kate Wright.

I appreciate my friends Netty Kahan, Amy Kahn, Eileen Olicker, Richard Posner, Pesha Ross, Chana Rutter, and Marian Sanders; and colleagues Linda Bloom, LCSW, Dorie Rosenberg, MFT, Sherrin Packer Rosenthal, MSW, and Pam Sweeney, MFT, for their suggestions and encouragement regarding the book. I am grateful to Stan Weisner, PhD, and Tom Nichols, PhD, both of whom recognized the value of marriage meetings and arranged for me to teach classes on the subject to psychotherapists and graduate students at the University of California Berkeley Extension and Alliant International University, San Francisco, respectively.

For endorsing an earlier, distilled version of this book,

Marriage Meeting Starter Kit, I thank Dr. Miriam Adahan; Joel Blackwell; Pamela Butler, PhD; Jon Carlson, PsyD, EdD; Adrian Fried; Chumi Friedman; Edward M. Hallowell, MD; Gay Hendricks, PhD; Shira Marin, MFT; Susan Page; Sarah Chana Radcliffe, MEd; Rabbi Yisrael Rice; and Rabbi Berel Wein.

I am grateful to Georgia Hughes, editorial director at New World Library, for her brilliant editing, collaboration, patience, and kindness; to managing editor Kristen Cashman, to copy editor Bonita Hurd, and to everyone on the team at New World Library for promptly, graciously, and meticulously handling more details than I'd ever dreamed were involved in publishing a book.

I thank consulting editor Alan Rinzler for his sound direction in developing this book initially and literary agent Katharine Sands for her generous guidance.

Long-term president of the Marin Branch of the California Writers Club Barbara Truax has earned accolades for her devoted, effective leadership. Members of the club Robert Haro and John Shearer also get a special "thank you" for their wise advice and encouragement.

My psychotherapy clients and couples at my Marriage Meeting workshops are essential to this book's existence. I am deeply grateful to all who have been willing to share aspects of their experiences.

For their astute contributions, I thank the psychotherapists and graduate students who attended my continuing education classes about marriage meetings and couple therapy.

I appreciate my sisters, Gloria Finkelstein and Marilyn Neugarten, for helping me to stay grounded, often with humor, during my new-book-author journey. I value my son, Avi Berger, for doing the same, and for adding so much joy to my life. I am eternally grateful to my parents, Mollie Herman Fisch Goldfarb and Oscar Fisch, both of blessed memory, for supporting me in all of my endeavors, and for encouraging me to take risks and to have fun.

Acknowledgments

My dear husband, David Berger, has been steadfast in his support, whether proofreading, providing editorial suggestions, or reminding me to turn off the computer and get some sleep. He has been a sounding board night and day about this book and most everything else. My cup runneth over.

Endnotes

Chapter 1. Marriage Meeting Basics

1. The concept of a marriage meeting has been mentioned briefly in other publications. The four-part agenda described here is modified from the one suggested in *Time for a Better Marriage*, by Don Dinkmeyer and Jon Carlson (Circle Pines, MN: American Guidance Service, 1984), 76.

Chapter 2. Debunking Marriage Myths

1. Ellen Kreidman, *Light His Fire* (Morton Grove, IL: Mega Systems, 1995), audiotape set.
2. This story is a highly paraphrased version that captures the essence of what actually happened as reported by Chana Sharfstein in "Searching the Novels for Perfect Love?" The Rebbe.org, undated, www.chabad.org/therebbe/article_cdo /aid/1218085/jewish/Searching-the-Novels-for-Perfect -Love.htm, accessed August 7, 2013.
3. John Gottman, *The Seven Principles for Making Marriage Work* (New York: Three Rivers Press, 1999).

Chapter 4. Coordinating Chores

1. A survey of 2,020 U.S. adults by the Pew Research Center concluded that "sharing household chores" is the third-most important factor in a successful marriage, behind faithfulness and a happy sexual relationship. Seventy-two percent of respondents assigned high importance to housework, which outranked even such necessities as adequate income and good housing. Moreover, a 2003 study by Scott Coltrane, a sociology professor at the University of California, Riverside, linked fathers' housework to more feelings of warmth and affection in their wives. And a survey of 288 husbands, reported in Neil Chethik's 2006 book *VoiceMale*, linked a wife's satisfaction with the division of household duties to her husband's satisfaction with their sex life. These details are from an article by Sue Shellenbarger, "Housework Pays Off between the Sheets," *Wall Street Journal*, October 21, 2009, http://online.wsj.com/news/articles/SB10001424052748704500060457448535163814731 2, accessed November 12, 2013.

2. *Prevention* magazine confirms the health benefits of making lists, including lists of chores. Nancy Kalish, "Why a To-Do List Keeps You Healthy," *Prevention* magazine's website, undated, www.smub.it/defz, accessed August 7, 2013.

Chapter 5. Planning for Good Times

1. Julia Cameron, *The Artist's Way* (New York: Jeremy P. Tarcher/Putnam, 1992), 18.

2. Ellen Kreidman, *Light His Fire* (Morton Grove, IL: Mega Systems, 1995), audiotape set.

Chapter 7. I-Statements

1. The formula for how to make an I-statement comes from "I Statements," Parenting Wisely website, undated, www.parenting

wisely.com/media/uploads/cms/pdf/I%20messages.pdf, accessed September 2, 2013.

Chapter 9. More Communication Techniques

1. Virginia Satir, *Conjoint Family Therapy*, 3rd ed. (Palo Alto, CA: Behavior Books, 1983).
2. A. Mehrabian and M. Wiener, "Decoding of Inconsistent Communications," *Journal of Personality and Social Psychology* 6 (1967): 109–14; and A. Mehrabian and S. R. Ferris, "Inference of Attitudes from Nonverbal Communication in Two Channels," *Journal of Consulting Psychology* 31, no. 3 (1967): 248–52. Other pertinent articles are listed on Mehrabian's website under "Personality and Communication: Psychological Books and Articles of Popular Interest," www.kaaj.com/psych.
3. Active listening instructions are adapted from Ralph Fry, Susan Mejia Johnson, Pete Melendez, and Dr. Roger Morgan, *Changing Destructive Adolescent Behavior: A Parent Workbook* (Rancho Cucamonga, CA: Parent Project, 2002), 141.

Chapter 13. Couple Progresses from Verbal Abuse to Healthier Relating

1. On a case-by-case basis, I evaluate my patients and determine when it is appropriate for me to provide individual psychotherapy to a partner who sees me for couple therapy. I view family members' behaviors as occurring within the context of a larger constellation, or system. In the case of a couple, I pay attention to how both partners cooperate unknowingly to perpetuate a relationship problem, for which one partner may blame the other. Marcia Fisch (a.k.a. Marcia Naomi Berger), "Homeostasis: A Key Concept in Working with Alcoholic Family Systems," *Family Therapy* 3, no. 2 (1976): 133–39, www.marcia naomiberger.com/wp-content/uploads/2010/10/Homeo

statis-A-Key-Concept-in-Working-With-Alcoholic-Families
.pdf.

Chapter 14. Marriage Meeting Techniques
Support Couple Therapy

1. Bill Herring, "Recovering from Infidelity: The Long and Winding Road," Bill Herring website, November 15, 2009, www.bill herring.info/atlanta_counseling/recovering-infidelity-long-and-winding-road.

Reading List

After you have finished *Marriage Meetings for Lasting Love: 30 Minutes a Week to the Relationship You've Always Wanted*, the best thing you can do is to put its teachings into practice by scheduling your first marriage meeting. For further reading, I recommend the following:

Berman, Claire. *Adult Children of Divorce Speak Out: About Growing Up with and Moving beyond Parental Divorce*. New York: Simon and Schuster, 1991.

Bloom, Linda, and Charlie Bloom. *101 Things I Wish I Knew When I Got Married: Simple Lessons to Make Love Last*. Novato, CA: New World Library, 2004.

Boteach, Shmuley. *Kosher Sex: A Recipe for Passion and Intimacy*. New York: Doubleday, 1999.

Brizendine, Louann. *The Female Brain*. New York: Broadway Books, 2007.

———. *The Male Brain*. New York: Broadway Books, 2010.

Butler, Pamela. *Self-Assertion for Women*. San Francisco: Harper-Collins, 1992.

————. *Talking to Yourself: How Cognitive Behavior Therapy Can Change Your Life.* Charleston, SC: BookSurge, 2008.

Cameron, Julia. *The Artist's Way.* New York: Jeremy P. Tarcher/Putnam, 1992.

Carlson, Jon, and Don Dinkmeyer. *Time for a Better Marriage: Training in Marriage Enrichment.* Rev. ed. Atascadero, CA: Impact, 2002.

Chapman, Gary. *The 5 Love Languages: The Secret to Love That Lasts.* Chicago: Northfield, 2009.

Feldman, Aharon. *The River, the Kettle and the Bird: A Torah Guide to Successful Marriage.* Spring Valley, NY: Feldheim, 1987.

Fisch, Marcia [Marcia Naomi Berger]. "Homeostasis: A Key Concept in Working with Alcoholic Family Systems." *Family Therapy* 3, no. 2 (1976): 133–39, www.marcianaomiberger.com/wp-content/uploads/2010/10/Homeostatis-A-Key-Concept-in-Working-With-Alcoholic-Families.pdf.

Gottman, John. *The Seven Principles for Making Marriage Work.* New York: Three Rivers Press, 1999.

————. *Why Marriages Succeed or Fail...And How You Can Make Yours Last.* New York: Fireside, 1995.

Graham, Linda. *Bouncing Back: Rewiring Your Brain for Maximum Resilience and Well-Being.* Novato, CA: New World Library, 2013.

Hallowell, Edward. *Crazy Busy.* New York: Ballantine, 2006.

Hendrix, Harville. *Getting the Love You Want: A Guide for Couples; 20th Anniversary Edition.* New York: Henry Holt, 2008.

Johnson, Sue. *Hold Me Tight: Seven Conversations for a Lifetime of Love.* New York: Little, Brown, 2008.

Kreidman, Ellen. *Light Her Fire.* New York: Dell, 1992. This and the next title are available as a CD set at www.lighthisfire.com/products.

————. *Light His Fire.* New York: Dell, 1991.

Pease, Barbara, and Allan Pease. *The Definitive Book of Body Language*. New York: Bantam Dell, 2006.

Satir, Virginia. *Conjoint Family Therapy*. 3rd ed. Palo Alto, CA: Behavior Books, 1983.

Tannen, Deborah. *You Just Don't Understand*. New York: Harper Paperbacks, 2001.

Wallerstein, Judith S., Julia M. Lewis, and Sandra Blakeslee. *The Unexpected Legacy of Divorce: A 25 Year Landmark Study*. New York: Hyperion, 2000.

Wallin, David J. *Attachment in Psychotherapy*. New York: Guilford Press, 2007.

Wile, Daniel B. *After the Honeymoon: How Conflict Can Improve Your Relationship*. Rev. ed. Hoboken, NJ: John Wiley and Sons, 1988.

———. *Couples Therapy: A Nontraditional Approach*. Hoboken, NJ: Wiley, 1992.

Index

About the Author

Marcia Naomi Berger (née Fisch), MSW, LCSW, leads dynamic marriage and communication workshops and is a popular speaker at conferences. In addition to working as a clinical social worker with a private psychotherapy practice in San Rafael, California, she teaches continuing education classes for psychotherapists and counselors at the University of California Berkeley Extension and Alliant International University in San Francisco.

While employed by the City and County of San Francisco, she held senior-level positions in the fields of child welfare, alcoholism treatment, and psychiatry. She also served as a lecturer on the clinical faculty at the University of California, San Francisco, School of Medicine, and as executive director of Jewish Family and Children's Services of the East Bay.

Marcia Naomi Berger lives in Marin County, California, with her husband, David Berger. She gives their weekly marriage meetings major credit for their happiness together and for her passion to share this tool with couples everywhere.

She may be contacted at mnaomiberger@gmail.com or through her website, www.marriagemeetings.com.